Telepathic Impressions
A Review and Report of Thirty-five New Cases

Telepathic Impressions

A Review and Report
Of Thirty-five New Cases

Ian Stevenson, M.D.

School of Medicine
University of Virginia

University Press of Virginia
Charlottesville
1970

CONTENTS

ACKNOWLEDGMENTS

Much of the early work on this study was carried out during my tenure of a Fellowship from the Commonwealth Fund in Zurich, Switzerland, and I extend grateful thanks to the Directors of the Fund for this support. Thanks are also due to the Parapsychology Foundation, Mrs. Eileen J. Garrett, President, for grants in support of my investigations in parapsychology.

Mr. and Mrs. Chester F. Carlson gave much valuable encouragement besides generous financial support for these investigations. In addition, I have profited greatly from discussions with Mrs. Carlson, herself a percipient on numerous occasions, about how the experiences described in this monograph seem to those having them.

To Mrs. Rosalind Heywood I am much indebted for her important contributions to the study of several of the cases, especially those of Mrs. Hellström. Mrs. Heywood also gave me information about one case (Case 10) and put me in touch with the percipient. In addition, she gave many valuable suggestions for the improvement of the entire monograph in its earlier stages.

Mrs. Mary Margaret Fuller kindly put me in touch with two of the percipients whose experiences I have studied. Mrs. Eva Hellström sent me information about one case (Case 26) and translated and transmitted my questions about it to the informant.

Mrs. Laura A. Dale was of invaluable help in searching the literature for cases of the type under consideration in this monograph; she also contributed her excellent judgment about the merits of the cases and her usual editorial skill. I am also grateful to Dr. J. G. Pratt for carefully reading the entire manuscript and offering helpful suggestions for its improvement.

For permission to quote from books published by them I wish to thank Rascher Verlag, Zurich, Switzerland, and Chatto and Windus, London.

Lastly, I extend thanks to the percipients and other informants of the new cases presented for their most helpful cooperation in furnishing testimony and answering so patiently all my questions about details.

I.S.

University of Virginia
October, 1969

Chapter One

INTRODUCTION

Most studies of spontaneous experiences suggestive of extrasensory perception have focused on cases which contain some kind of sensory imagery rather than on those which merely involve simple "impressions" or "intuitions" about a distant person.[1] This is natural enough, for such impressions are harder to verify and analyze because they include no detailed images to compare with the related events. Yet in L. E. Rhine's large collection of spontaneous experiences, impression cases (49), or "intuitive" cases, as she calls them, form more than 25 per cent of the total (1839 out of 7119). In the smaller survey of the Society for Psychical Research (S.P.R.), at least 15 per cent of the total (46 out of 300) cases were imageless impressions (17); and in a large German series of a thousand cases, impressions (*Ahnungen*) accounted for more than 26 per cent (56, 57). In a more recent survey of spontaneous psychical experiences among Indian school children, impression cases provided almost 32 per cent of the total (41). The Indian survey was particularly important in indicating the frequency of impression cases (at least in one culture) since all the children

---

[1] I prefer to characterize these cases as "impressions" rather than "intuitions" because the latter word usually implies a more or less definite cognitive experience, whereas the word "impression" leaves us free to consider a wider range of cases, including those with only changes in emotions or physical symptoms or involving some impulsive action. The percipients themselves seem to use the two words with about equal frequency to describe their experiences.

surveyed were obliged to respond to the questionnaire about spontaneous experiences. This contrasts with the other surveys, which depended upon reports of experiences voluntarily submitted to the investigating institution. Table 1 summarizes the data on the incidence of impression and other types of experiences in these four surveys. From their frequency alone, imageless impressions suggestive of extrasensory perception deserve much further study.

Table 1

TYPES OF ESP EXPERIENCES IN SPONTANEOUS CASES
SURVEYS FROM DIFFERENT COUNTRIES
(Percentages Only)

Type of Experience	American Series (49) N=7119	German Series (56, 57) N=1000	English Series (17) N=300	Indian Series (41) N=900
Dreams	64.6	63.0	37.0	52.4
Waking Sensory Images or Hallucinations	9.6	10.3	39.0	15.7
Waking Impression or Intuitive Experiences	25.8	26.7	15.0	31.9
Indeterminate	0	0	9.0	0

To orient the reader to the type of case under review in this monograph, I shall now cite four older impression cases, taking one from each of the four main sources of the authenticated cases which I shall be reviewing in Chapter II.

OLDER ILLUSTRATIVE CASES

The first case is taken from *Phantasms of the Living*. The percipient, Mr. James Carroll, described his experience in a communication dated July, 1884, as follows:

> I beg to forward my experience of about six years ago, while living in the employment of Colonel Turbervill, near Bridgend, Glamorgan, and a twin brother in the same capacity with a lady at Chobham Place, Bagshot, Surrey.

I may mention that my brother and I were devotedly attached from children, and our resemblance to each other so remarkable that only one or two of our family then living, and oldest friends, could distinguish any difference between us. Up to June 17th, 1878, I had not known my brother to have one day's illness, and in consequence of having about this time recovered heavy financial loss, there was this and other unusual cause for cheerfulness. But on the morning of the date given, about half-past 11, I experienced a *strange sadness* and depression. Unable to account for it, I turned to my desk, thinking of my brother. I looked at his last letter to see the date, and tried to detect if there was anything unusual in it, but failed. I wrote off to my brother, closed my desk, and felt compelled to exclaim quite aloud, "My brother or I will break down." This I afterwards found was the first day of his fatal illness.

I wrote again to him, but in consequence of his being ill I received no reply. We usually wrote twice a-week. I tried to persuade myself his silence was due to being busy. On the following Saturday, the 22nd, while speaking to Mr. Turbervill, a sudden depression, which I had never before realised, and which I feel impossible to describe, came over me. I felt strange and unwell. I retired as soon as possible, thankful my state of mind had not been noticed. I would have gone to my room, but felt it might be noticed, and felt frightened too, as if something might suddenly happen to me.

I went, instead, into the footman's pantry, where they were cleaning the place, and sat down, suppressed my feelings, but alluded to a dulness and concern for my brother. I was speaking, when a messenger entered with a telegram to announce my brother's dangerous state, and requesting my immediate presence. He died on the following Monday morning. It is clearly proved that at the time I felt the melancholy described he was speaking of me in great distress. We were never considered superstitious, and I was never apt to feelings of melancholy. . . .

In reply to inquiries, Mr. Carroll wrote further details, on August 8, 1884, as follows:

I find it difficult now, after the lapse of time and many changes, to get the memory of friends to recall the subjects of our correspondence. I left South Wales on the death of my brother, and have been moving about among strangers ever since; circumstances on this part of the matter are singularly against me.

You asked in your previous letter, Was the impression of distress and apprehension which I described, rare to me in my experience? I never before felt anything like it, except in a milder form, before the death of my mother, about 14 years ago, while I was at Lord Robarts' seat in Arnhill, and my mother in London. The sensation then was about two or three days previous to her death. I have always been an opponent to ghost theory, and till my brother's death I never thought to entertain the idea that there could be any unseen power in the thought of apparitions.

My brother's death was from a cold neglected, and inflammation rapidly setting in. We were twins, his age at time of death 39 about. From our extraordinary resemblance we were well known. I may mention my brother being the only near relation left.

I sent to Ireland for signatures to a distant relative, who was with me as an adopted son shortly after my brother's death, for about two years. He is about 18 years of age; his name, too, is James Carroll. His corroboration comes very close to the time.

An old friend, of 25 years, 30 I think, holding a good position in one of our chief banking houses, also promised to corroborate, a day or two ago. I enclose now a note from him, just received. He remembers the subject. I often, just after my brother's death, spoke of it to him.

On August 10, 1884, a nephew and namesake of Mr. Carroll's wrote as follows:

I hereby certify that Mr. Carroll frequently, during the early part of my residence with him, about 5 years ago, spoke of the presentiment he describes in a letter written to you, a copy of which he has sent me.

The following is a letter, dated August 16, 1884, to Mr. Carroll from a friend, Mr. James Martin:

. . . From the time of your brother's death till the present, I have spent much time in your society. I remember well the account you gave me of the dreadful depression of mind you passed through just previous to his death. It was singular, but true (18, Vol. 1, pp. 281-282; case 5 of Tabulation[2]).

Mr. Carroll also furnished a letter written by Mrs. Benyan, his brother's employer, at the time when the brother was dangerously ill. The letter was to a solicitor and expressed a desire that he, James Carroll, should be informed of the illness. The letter proved that the illness was sudden and that Mr. Carroll was unaware of it.

The next case was investigated by Hodgson and reported by Myers in *Proc.* S.P.R. The percipient, Mrs. C. A. C. Hadselle, wrote to Hodgson on May 28, 1888, as follows:

> Less than two years ago a curious thing happened to me. I had been in Wash. Co., N.Y., giving half a dozen readings, and was on my way to Williamstown, where I had spent a part of the summer, and where much of my worldly goods, in the shape of wearing apparel, was safely stowed in my room at the "Mansion House." With ticket purchased, I was serenely seated in the car, "box, bundle and bag" beside me, the conductor's "All aboard" was at that instant in my ears, when I sprang to my feet with the force of an inward command, "Change your ticket and go to Elizabeth (N.J.). *Change your ticket and go to Elizabeth.* Change your—" Here a gentleman in the opposite seat—an utter stranger—rose and said: "Madam, have you forgotten something, can I help you?" I said: "Do you think the train will wait for me to change my ticket?" For there appeared to be no alternative. As I spoke I moved towards the platform; he followed, and seeing that the office was but a few steps distant said: "Go, I'll see that you are not left." I did go, and in a moment more was on my way to Elizabeth, *though I had not before even thought of such a thing.* Next morning, on reaching my friend's house, she threw her arms about me and sobbed out: "Oh, I have wanted you so." Then she led me to a room where an only and beloved sister lay in life's last battle. In an hour it was ended.
>
> My poor grief-stricken friend declared then—declares now— that my sudden change of purpose was a direct answer to her re-

---

[2] The Tabulation appears on the pages that follow.

TABULATION

No. of Case	Published Source[1]	Sex of Percipient	Sex of Apparent Agent	Relationship of Percipient to Agent	Condition of Agent	Agent Focusing on Percipient	Percipient Alone or With Others[2]	Number of Additional Details	Action Taken by Percipient	Agent Identified by Percipient	Emotion of Percipient[3]	Remarks
1	PL, Vol. I p. 271	M	F	Brother	Dying	Unknown	Alone*	0	No	No	Dread	
2	PL, Vol. I p. 273	F	M	Wife	Ill	Unknown	Alone	0	No	No	Not stated	Percip. felt faint; thought she was dying
3	PL, Vol. I p. 277	F	M	Wife	Dying; In delirium	Yes	Alone	0	Yes	No	Depressed	Percip. weeping; restless
4	PL, Vol. I pp. 278-9	M	M	Son	Dying	Unknown	With others	0	No	No	Depressed	
5	PL, Vol. I pp. 281-2	M	M	Twin brother	Fatally ill	Yes	Unknown	0	Yes	Yes	Sadness	Percip. felt unwell
6	PL, Vol. I p. 283	M	M	Twin brother	In danger of drowning	Unknown	Unknown	0	No	Yes	Not stated	
7	PL, Vol. I pp. 283-4	M	M	Son	Dying	Unknown	With others	0	Yes	Yes	Great anxiety	
8	PL, Vol. I p. 284	F	M	Wife	Dying	Unknown	With others	0	Yes	No	Not stated	Auditory component
9	PL, Vol. I pp. 285-6	M	F	Husband	Seriously injured	Yes	With others	0	Yes	No	Uneasy	Pure motor effect
10	PL, Vol. I pp. 286-7	F	M	Daughter	Dying	Yes	With others	0	Yes	No	Not stated	
11	PL, Vol. I p. 287	M	M	Son	Dying	Unknown	With others	0	Yes	No	Not stated	
12	PL, Vol. I pp. 287-8	F	M	Wife	Dangerously ill	Yes	With others	0	Yes	Yes	Not stated	
13	PL, Vol. I pp. 288-9	M	M	Son	Grieving	Yes	Unknown	0	Yes	No	Not stated	
14	PL, Vol. I pp. 291-2	M	M	Friend	Ill	No	Alone	0	Yes	Yes	Disturbed	

	Source[1]						Alone[2]					
15	PL, Vol. II p. 350	M	M	Friend	Dying	Unknown	Alone	1	No	Yes	Not stated	Percip. very ill at time of experience
16	PL, Vol. II pp. 350-51	M	M	Father	Dying	Unknown	Alone	1	No	Yes	Not stated	Percip. dying at time of experience
17	PL, Vol. II p. 353	M	M	Son	Dying	Unknown	With others	1	Yes	Yes	Depressed	Percip. committed suicide
18	PL, Vol. II pp. 354-5	M	M	Brother	Dying	Yes	With others	1	No	Yes	Very unpleasant feeling; anxiety	
19	PL, Vol. II p. 356	F	M	Mother	Lost	Unknown	With others	1	No	Yes	Very uneasy	
20	PL, Vol. II pp. 356-8	M	F	Friend	Seriously ill	Unknown	Unknown	0	No	Yes	Not stated	
21	PL, Vol. II pp. 360-61	F	F	Sister	Danger of fire	Unknown	Alone*	0	Yes	Yes	Exceedingly uneasy	
22	PL, Vol. II p. 363	F	M	Mother	Arrival	Yes	Unknown	1	Yes	Yes	Not stated	
23	PL, Vol. II p. 364	F	F	Friend	Arrival	Yes	With others	1	No	Yes	Not stated	
24	PL, Vol. II pp. 364-5	F	M	Stranger	Not in trouble	No	Alone	0	Yes	No	Not stated	
25	PL, Vol. II p. 365	F	M	Acquaintance	Not in trouble	Unknown	With others	0	No	Yes	Distressed	
26	PL, Vol. II pp. 370-71	M	M	Father	Ill	Unknown	Alone	0	Yes	Yes	Restless and uneasy	
27	PL, Vol. II p. 371	M	M	Friend	In danger of drowning	Unknown	Unknown	0	Yes	Yes	Not stated	Percip. prayed

[1]The following abbreviations are used for sources: PL, **Phantasms of the Living;** PSPR, **Proceedings** of the Society for Psychical Research; JSPR, **Journal** of the Society for Psychical Research; JASPR, **Journal** of the American Society for Psychical Research; BuSPR, **Bulletin** of the Boston Society for Psychic Research.

[2]An asterisk (*) in this column indicates that the percipient was asleep at the onset of the experience; unless so noted, the percipient was awake.

[3]In almost all instances, the words descriptive of emotion are quoted verbatim from the original reports.

No. of Case	Published Source	Sex of Percipient	Sex of Apparent Agent	Relationship of Percipient to Agent	Condition of Agent	Agent Focusing on Percipient	Percipient Alone or With Others	Number of Additional Details	Action Taken by Percipient	Agent Identified by Percipient	Emotion of Percipient	Remarks
28	PL, Vol. II pp. 371-2	M	M	Friend	Dying	Unknown	Alone	0	Yes	Yes	Feeling of strange horror	Percip. felt he was coming down with bad illness.
29	PL, Vol. II p. 374	F	M	Mother	In accident	Unknown	Unknown	0	Yes	Yes	Uncontrollable apprehension	
30	PL, Vol. II pp. 374-5	M	F	Son	Dying	Unknown	Alone	0	Yes	No	Depressed	Percip. felt he would die
31	PL, Vol. II pp. 375-6	M	M	Friend	Dying	Unknown	With others	0	No	No	Restless and uneasy	
32	PL, Vol. II pp. 376-7	M	F	Son	In danger from fire	Yes	With others	0	Yes	No	Not stated	Automatic behavior
33	PL, Vol. II p. 377	M	F	Acquaintance	Ill	Yes	With others	0	Yes	No	Continuous pressure	
34	PL, Vol. II pp. 377-8	M	M	Father	In danger from fire	Unknown	With others	0	Yes	No	Not stated	Pure motor effect
35	PSPR, Vol. 1 p. 31	F	M	Wife	In accident	Unknown	With others	1	No	Yes	Anxious	
36	PSPR, Vol. 1 pp. 31-32	F	F	Daughter	Dying	Yes	Alone*	1	Yes	Yes	Frightened	Sister also a percip.
37	PSPR, Vol. 1 p. 59	M	M	Father	In accident	Unknown	With others	0	No	Yes	Depressed	
38	PSPR, Vol. 2 p. 122	M	M	Twin brother	Dying	Unknown	Alone	0	Yes	No	Frightened	Percip. felt ill; convinced he was dying
39	PSPR, Vol. 2 pp. 122-3	M	F	Grandson	Ill	Yes	Alone*	0	No	No	Dismal wretchedness; deep melancholy	Percip. also noted an abatement in his depression at time agent improved
40	PSPR, Vol. 2 pp. 132-3	M	M	Brother	Arrival	Unknown	Unknown	1	Yes	Yes	Not stated	

No.	Reference	Sex	Sex	Relationship	Needing help		Alone/With others		Warm relationship	Crisis	Emotion	Remarks
41	PSPR, Vol. 6 p. 364	F	F	Friend	In accident	Unknown	Unknown	0	Yes	Yes	Not stated	
42	PSPR, Vol. 7 p. 38	M	M	Son		Unknown	With others	0	No	Yes	Not stated	
43	PSPR, Vol. 9 pp. 33-5	F	F	Friend	Friend's sister dying	Yes	With others	0	Yes	Yes	Not stated	
44	PSPR, Vol. 9 pp. 37-8	F	F	Friend	Dying	Unknown	With others	0	Yes	Yes	Not stated	
45	PSPR, Vol. 10 pp. 131-2	F	M	Daughter	Dying	Unknown	Alone	0	No	No	Foreboding of evil	Percip. also felt as if someone grasped her arm
46	PSPR, Vol. 10 pp. 258-9	F	M	Sister	Dying	Unknown	With others	0	Yes	Yes	Not stated	Percip. prayed
47	PSPR, Vol. 12 pp. 33-4	M	M	Stranger	Robbing percip.	Unknown	Alone*	1	Yes	No	Not stated	
48	PSPR, Vol. 12 pp. 275-6	F	M	Sister	Ill	Unknown	Unknown	0	No	Yes	Not stated	
49	PSPR, Vol. 53 p. 153	F	F	Mother-in-law	Labor pains	Yes	With others	0	No	No	Not stated	Pain case
50	PSPR, Vol. 53 pp. 159-60	F	M	Mother	Bleeding	Unknown	With others	0	Yes	Yes	Not stated	Percip. unable to sit still; 2 agents possible
51	JSPR, Vol. 1 pp. 54-5	F	F	Sister	Anxious	Unknown	Unknown	0	No	No	Cloud of calamity wrapping me around	
52	JSPR, Vol 1 pp. 81-2	M	F	Friend (Fiancé)	Dying	Unknown	Unknown	0	Yes	Yes	Not stated	
53	JSPR, Vol. 1 pp. 82-3	F	M	Wife	In accident	Unknown	Alone	1	No	Yes	Sadness	Percip. wept and trembled

No. of Case	Published Source	Sex of Percipient	Sex of Apparent Agent	Relationship of Percipient to Agent	Condition of Agent	Agent Focusing on Percipient	Percipient Alone or With Others	Number of Additional Details	Action Taken by Percipient	Agent Identified by Percipient	Emotion of Percipient	Remarks
54	JSPR, Vol. 1 p. 95	F	M	Mother	Dying	Unknown	With others	0	No	Yes	Not stated	
55	JSPR, Vol. 1 p. 102	F	M	Friend	Dying	Unknown	Alone*	1	Yes	Yes	Not stated	
56	JSPR, Vol. 1 p. 105	F	M	Friend	Seriously ill	Yes	With others	1	Yes	Yes	Not stated	
57	JSPR, Vol. 1 pp. 365-6	F	M	Daughter	Dying	Yes	With others	0	No	No	Intense sadness	Percip. in "hysterics"
58	JSPR, Vol. 1 pp. 366-7	F	F	Cousin	Dying	Unknown	Alone	1	No	No	Anxious	Percip. felt weak; felt she was dying
59	JSPR, Vol. 1 pp. 384-5	M	F	Cousin	Dying	Unknown	With others	1	No	Yes	Not stated	
60	JSPR, Vol. 1 pp. 435-6	F	M	Cousin	Dying	Unknown	With others	1	No	Yes	Not stated	
61	JSPR, Vol. 1 pp. 485-6	F	M	Mother	In accident	Unknown	With others	1	No	Yes	Not stated	
62	JSPR, Vol. 2 p. 18	F	F	Acquaintance	Dying	Yes	Unknown	0	Yes	Yes	Anxiety (sleepless)	Two percips. involved
63	JSPR, Vol. 2 p. 69	M	F	Son	Seriously ill	Yes	Alone*	0	Yes	Yes	Peculiar yearning	
64	JSPR, Vol. 2 pp. 76-7	M	F	Husband	Dying	Unknown	With others	0	No	No	Fearful depression of spirits	
65	JSPR, Vol. 2 p. 78	F	M	Sister	Severely depressed	Unknown	With others	0	Yes	No	Uneasiness; restlessness	
66	JSPR, Vol. 3 p. 268	M	F	Nephew	Dying	Unknown	With others	0	No	No	Vivid sense of presence of death	Percip. thought person other than agent had died
67	JSPR, Vol. 4 pp. 179-81	F	M	Friend	Proposing marriage	Yes	Alone	1	No	Yes	"Good news," but emotion not stated	

68	JSPR, Vol.4 pp.269-70	F	F	Sister	Dying	Unknown	With others	0	No	No	Very sad, "grief and sorrow"	Percip. cried bitterly
69	JSPR, Vol.4 pp.291-2	F	F	Friend	Arrival	Yes	With others	1	Yes	Yes	Not stated	
70	JSPR, Vol.5 pp.137-8	F	F	Friend	Dying	Unknown	With others	0	Yes	Yes	Not stated	Automatic behavior—playing piano
71	JSPR, Vol.5 p.172	M	F	Son	Needing shawl	No	Alone	1	Yes	Yes	Not stated	
72	JSPR, Vol.5 p.241	M	M	Twin brother	Dying	Unknown	Unknown	1	No	Yes	Not stated	Percip. had an attack of jaundice
73	JSPR, Vol.6 pp.101-2	M	M	Son	Dying	Unknown	With others	0	Yes	No	Feeling of horror	Percip.'s wife also a percip.
74	JSPR, Vol.6 pp.163-5	M	F	Husband	In accident	Yes	Alone	0	No	Yes	Tinge of uneasiness	
75	JSPR, Vol.6 pp.184-5	F	M	Friend	In accident	Unknown	With others	0	Yes	Yes	In good spirits, but startled	Percip. also had tactile sensations
76	JSPR, Vol.7 pp.101-3	F	F	Acquaintance	Dying	Unknown	With others	0	No	No	Not stated	Two other percips. involved
77	JSPR, Vol.7 pp.120-21	F	M	Sister	Ill	Unknown	Unknown	0	No	No	Dread; possessed with terror	
78	JSPR, Vol.7 pp.195-6	F	M	Wife	Had just lost money	No	With others	2	No	Yes	Not stated	Percip. had queer sensation like electric shock
79	JSPR, Vol.8 pp.10-12	F	F	Aunt	In danger of fire	Unknown	Alone	1	No	Yes	Miserable frame of mind; horror and fright	

No. of Case	Published Source	Sex of Percipient	Sex of Apparent Agent	Relationship of Percipient to Agent	Condition of Agent	Agent Focusing on Percipient	Percipient Alone or With Others	Number of Additional Details	Action Taken by Percipient	Agent Identified by Percipient	Emotion of Percipient	Remarks
80	JSPR, Vol. 8 pp. 125-8	M	F	Son	Dying	Unknown	With others	0	Yes	Yes	Not stated	
81	JSPR, Vol. 8 pp. 192-3	F	F	Acquaintance	Arrival	Yes	With others	0	No	Yes	Not stated	
82	JSPR, Vol. 8 p. 266	M	M	Son	Dying	Unknown	Alone	0	Yes	No	Appalling fear	
83	JSPR, Vol. 8 p. 308	M	F	Husband	Possible danger of fire	Unknown	Alone	1	No	Yes	Anxious	Percip.'s sister also a possible percip.
84	JSPR, Vol. 9 p. 32	M	F	Husband	Ill	Unknown	Unknown	1	Yes	Yes	Not stated	
85	JSPR, Vol. 11 p. 315-20	F	F	Friend	Friend's mother fatally ill	Yes	Alone	2	Yes	No	Depressed	Automatic behavior
86	JSPR, Vol. 14 pp. 99-100	F	M	Friend	Ill	Unknown	With others	1	No	Yes	Not stated	
87	JSPR, Vol. 16 pp. 203-5	M	F	Friend	Dying	Unknown	With others	0	No	Yes	Not stated	Two agents possible
88	JSPR, Vol. 18 pp. 56-8	F	M	Cousin	In anxious state	Yes	Alone	2	No	Yes	Not stated	
89	JSPR, Vol. 22 pp. 122-3	F	M	Friend	Arrival	Unknown	With others	0	No	Yes	Not stated	
90	JSPR, Vol. 27 pp. 3-4	F	F	Friend	Dying	Unknown	Unknown	2	No	No	Feeling of disturbance	
91	JSPR, Vol. 28 pp. 156-7	M	F	Son	Needing help	Yes	With others*	0	Yes	Yes	Not stated	Another percip. involved
92	JSPR, Vol. 28 pp. 237-9	F	M	Sister	Seriously ill	Unknown	Alone	0	Yes	Yes	Unstrung	
93	JSPR, Vol. 28 pp. 258-9	F	M	Mother	Worried; needed money	Unknown	With others	1	Yes	Yes	Not stated	

#	Reference	F	M		Arrival			4	Yes	Yes?	Not stated	
94	JSPR, Vol. 38 pp. 248-9	F	M	Wife	Labor pains	Unknown	With others	0	Yes	Yes?	Not stated	Pain case
95	JSPR, Vol. 42 pp. 187-9	F	F	Mother		Yes	With others	0	No	No	Not stated	
96	JASPR, Vol. 3 pp. 419-22	F	F	Niece	Dying	Unknown	Unknown	0	No	No	Not stated	
97	JASPR, Vol. 3 pp. 626-7	F	F	Friend	In trouble	Yes	Unknown	0	Yes	Yes	Not stated	
98	JASPR, Vol. 8 pp. 123-5	F	M	Servant	Ill	Yes	With others	0	Yes	Yes	Not stated	
99	JASPR, Vol. 8 pp. 126-7	F	F	Acquaint-ance	Ill	Yes	Unknown	0	Yes	Yes	Not stated	
100	JASPR, Vol. 8 pp. 145-6	M	M	Brother	Dying	Unknown	Alone	0	No	Yes	Unusually un-happy; restless	
101	JASPR, Vol. 8 pp. 149-53	M	M	Father	Dying	Unknown	Alone	0	Yes	No	Awe; dread; foreboding	Possibly two or more percips.
102	JASPR, Vol. 8 pp. 197-8	F	F	Daughter	Ill	Yes	Unknown	0	Yes	Yes	Not stated	
103	JASPR, Vol. 8 pp. 203-4	M	M	Husband	Ill	Yes	Unknown	0	Yes	Yes	Not stated	
104	JASPR, Vol. 8 pp. 204-5	M	F	Acquaint-ance (doctor)	Ill	Yes	Alone	0	Yes	Yes	Not stated	
105	JASPR, Vol. 8 pp. 536-42	F	F	Sister	Dying	Unknown	Alone	0	No	No	Joyful	
106	JASPR, Vol. 12 pp. 251-5	F	M	Stranger	Robbing percip.	Unknown	With others	0	Yes	No	Not stated	

No. of Case	Published Source	Sex of Percipient	Sex of Apparent Agent	Relationship of Percipient to Agent	Condition of Agent	Agent Focusing on Percipient	Percipient Alone or With Others	Number of Additional Details	Action Taken by Percipient	Agent Identified by Percipient	Emotion of Percipient	Remarks
107	JASPR, Vol. 13 pp. 269-71	F	M	Wife	Anxious about son	Unknown	With others	0	Yes	Yes	Anxious; nervous; apprehensive	
108	JASPR, Vol. 15 pp. 378-80	M	M	Friend	Dying	Unknown	Unknown	1	Yes	Yes	Torn with anxiety	
109	JASPR, Vol. 15 pp. 394-6	M	M	Friend	Arrival	Unknown	Alone	0	Yes	Yes	Not stated	
110	JASPR, Vol. 18 pp. 141-3	M	M	Son	In accident	Yes	Alone	1	Yes	No	Uneasiness; fear	
111	JASPR, Vol. 19 pp. 20-23	F	F	Sister	Dying	Unknown	With others	0	No	No	Exceedingly nervous	
112	JASPR, Vol. 35 pp. 133-43	M	M	Son	Dying	Unknown	With others	1	No	Yes	Grief	Percip. sobbing; almost hysterical
113	JASPR, Vol. 40 pp. 59-63	M	M	Father	Dying	Unknown	With others	0	Yes	No	Anxious; restless; depressed	
114	JASPR, Vol. 40 pp. 74-6	M	F	Friend	Child ill	Unknown	Alone	1	No	Yes	Not stated	
115	JASPR, Vol. 40 p. 88	F	M	Daughter	Dying	Unknown	Alone	0	No	No	Not stated	Physical pain experienced
116	JASPR, Vol. 40 p. 90	M	F	Friend	In accident	Unknown	Alone*	1	Yes	Yes	Not stated	
117	JASPR, Vol. 45 pp. 98-9	F	F	Mother	Ill; frightened	Yes	Unknown	0	Yes	Yes	Not stated	
118	JASPR, Vol. 46 pp. 31-2	F	M	Niece	Dying	Unknown	Unknown	0	No	No	Not stated (percip. small child)	Percip. sobbed hysterically
119	JASPR, Vol. 48 pp. 43-5	F	F	Daughter	Dying	Unknown	With others	0	Yes	Yes	Anxious	Percip. had uncontrollable crying fit

120	JASPR, Vol. 49 pp. 86-7	M	F	Husband	Dying	Yes	Alone	1	Yes	Yes	Not stated	Two agents possible
121	JASPR, Vol. 50 pp. 158-61	F	M	Daughter	Dying	Unknown	Alone*	0	No	No	Sense of confusion	Percip. wept
122	JASPR, Vol. 52 pp. 24-34	M	M	Friend	Suffocating	Yes	Alone	0	Yes	No	Uneasy feeling	
123	JASPR, Vol. 56 pp. 32-4	F	F	Daughter	Unhappy, needing money	Yes	Unknown	1	Yes	Yes	Disturbed	
124	JASPR, Vol. 56 pp. 43-6	M	M	Friend	In danger of drowning	No	With others	0	Yes	Yes	Fear	Percip. prayed for agent
125	BuBSPR, #9 pp. 46-7	M	M	Friend	Dying	Unknown	Alone	0	No	Yes	Feeling of confusion	Percip. trembled
126	BuBSPR, #9 pp. 56-7	M	M	Acquaintance	Worried	Unknown	Alone	1	No	No	Troubled	
127	BuBSPR, #9 pp. 59-62	F	M	Stranger	Dying	No	Alone*	1	No	Yes	Not stated	
128	BuBSPR, #14 pp. 162-3	F	M	Sister	Dying	Unknown	Alone*	1	No	Yes	Fear	
129	BuBSPR, #14 pp. 244-5	F	M	Sister-in-law	Dying	Unknown	With others	1	No	Yes	Not stated	Percip. unable to sleep
130	BuBSPR, #14 pp. 245-6	M	M	Twin brother	Dying	Unknown	With others	1	Yes	Yes	Not stated	Percip. walked the floor all night
131	BuBSPR, #14 pp. 246-7	M	F	Friend	Dying	Unknown	Alone	1	Yes	Yes	Not stated	
132	BuBSPR, #14 pp. 250-51	M	M	Son	Dying	Unknown	With others	1	No	Yes	Not stated	
133	BuBSPR, #14 p. 251	F	F	Daughter	Dying	Unknown	Alone*	0	No	Yes	Not stated	Percip. wept

No. of Case	Published Source	Sex of Percipient	Sex of Apparent Agent	Relationship of Percipient to Agent	Condition of Agent	Agent Focusing on Percipient	Percipient Alone or With Others	Number of Additional Details	Action Taken by Percipient	Agent Identified by Percipient	Emotion of Percipient	Remarks
134	BuBSPR, #14 p. 255	M	F	Son	Dying	Unknown	Unknown	0	No	Yes	Fear	A number of other percips. were involved
135	BuBSPR, #14 p. 261	M	F	Son	Had just died	Unknown	With others	0	Yes	No	Not stated	
136	BuBSPR, #14 p. 262	M	M	Friend	Dying	Unknown	With others	0	Yes	No	Not stated	
137	BuBSPR, #14 pp. 262-3	M	M	Son	Dying	Unknown	Alone*	2	Yes	No	Not stated	Percip. unable to eat; food tasted bitter
138	BuBSPR, #14 pp. 263-4	M	M	Son	Dying	Yes	With others	0	No	No	Nervous and oppressed	
139	BuBSPR, #14 pp. 264-5	F	M	Daughter	Dying	Unknown	With others	0	No	No	Depressed	Percip. wept; another percip. also involved
140	BuBSPR, #14 pp. 268-9	F	M	Sister	Head injury	Unknown	Alone	1	No	Yes	Very depressed	Percip. felt severe blow on head
141	BuBSPR, #14 pp. 269-70	F	M	Mother	In accident	Unknown	With others	1	No	Yes	Not stated	Percip. walked the floor, wringing hands
142	BuBSPR, #14 pp. 270-71	M	F	Friend	Ill	Unknown	Alone	0	Yes	Yes	Not stated	Auditory component
143	BuBSPR, #14 pp. 272-3	F	M	Mother	Ill	Unknown	Unknown	0	Yes	No	Not stated	
144	BuBSPR, #14 p. 273	F	M	Mother	Danger of injury	Unknown	With others	1	No	Yes	Not stated	
145	BuBSPR, #14 pp. 273-4	F	M	Wife	Frightened	Unknown	Unknown	1	No	Yes	Not stated	
146	BuBSPR, #14 pp. 274-5	M	M	Brother	In danger of drowning	Yes	Alone*	0	Yes	Yes	Feeling of horror	

147	BuBSPR, #14 pp. 275-6	F	M	Sister	In accident	Unknown	With others	0	No	Yes	Not stated	
148	BuBSPR, #14 pp. 276-7	M	F	Husband	Needing help	Yes	With others	1	Yes	Yes	Not stated	
149	BuBSPR, #14 pp. 277-8	F	M	Sister	Worried	Unknown	With others	1	No	Yes	Not stated	
150	BuBSPR, #14 p. 279	F	F	Acquaintance	Ill	Unknown	Alone*	2	No	Yes	Not stated	
151	BuBSPR, #14 p. 282	F	M	Mother	Ill	Yes	Unknown	1	No	Yes	Not stated	
152	BuBSPR, #14 pp. 285-6	F	M	Mother	Ill	Unknown	Alone*	0	Yes	No	Not stated	2 agents possibly involved
153	BuBSPR, #14 pp. 286-7	M	F	Husband	In accident	Yes	Unknown	0	Yes	Yes	Not stated	
154	BuBSPR, #14 pp. 287-8	M	M	Father	Injured in accident	Unknown	Unknown	0	Yes	No	Not stated	2 agents possibly involved
155	BuBSPR, #14 p. 290	M	F	Husband	Undergoing surgery	Unknown	Alone*	0	Yes	No	Deep depression	Percip. prayed
156	BuBSPR, #14 pp. 291-2	F	M	Wife	Ill (arrival)	Unknown	With others	1	No	Yes	Not stated	
157	BuBSPR, #20 p. 19	F	M	Mother	In accident—in a faint	Yes	Unknown	0	No	Yes	Not stated	Reciprocal case
158	BuBSPR, #20 pp. 33-4	M	M	Friend	Dead	Unknown	With others	0	No	No	Not stated	
159	BuBSPR, #20 p. 51	M	F	Husband	Arrival	Unknown	Unknown	1	No	Yes	Not stated	
160	BuBSPR, #20 pp. 59-60	M	M	Friend	Wanting job (arrival)	Yes	Unknown	2	No	Yes	Not stated	

peated though unspoken demand for my presence. And who shall say it was not? I wish to add that while I had learned by letter of the sister's illness of a chronic disorder, I did not suppose her case hopeless; indeed, from the fact that no tidings had reached me lately, was hoping that she was on the road to recovery, and had I been questioned concerning her that 10th of November, 1886, should have replied confidently, "She will without doubt last through the winter." My friend, by the way, is, much more than I, a believer in psychical phenomena.

Mrs. G., the friend referred to by the percipient, sent Hodgson her corroboration, dated March 5, 1890. The incident occurred, she stated, on November 11, 1886. She said:

> I had not expected Mrs. H; did not at that time know where she was, so could not have summoned her had I wished to do so, —but in my trouble there grew upon me a great desire for her presence, and I said many times, "If she would only come. If she were only here."
>
> My sister's failure at the last was somewhat rapid, but of this Mrs. H. knew nothing, and when she told me of her sudden change of purpose, hundreds of miles away, I said: "The impulse was sent you in answer to my wish," or words to that effect.

The Rev. James Wilson, the gentleman on the train who helped the percipient to change her ticket, responded on March 20, 1890 to Hodgson's inquiries as follows:

> I recollect the circumstance of "assisting a lady" at Greenwich ticket office, who exchanged her ticket at the last moment, because of a change of purpose; and it was in November, 1886. She sent me a few lines afterwards, detailing certain facts touching a sick friend at the point of her destination—not clearly recalled at this moment (35, pp. 33-35; case 43 of Tabulation).

The next case was reported by W. F. Prince in *Human Experiences*. It was sent to Prince by "Professor CN, college president and Friend":

> This incident occurred when I was probably about fourteen years of age, though I may have been a year or two older or

younger. My father, mother and five younger children were living at Traverse City, Michigan, and my oldest sister and my oldest brother were living in a lumber town called Empire on the shore of Lake Michigan, approximately thirty miles from Traverse City. Empire at that time had no telephone or telegraph service, the only *regular* communication with the outside world being by means of a stage line, with communication by boat on occasion with Chicago and other lake ports.

My mother went to Empire for a week's visit with the families of this oldest sister and this oldest brother of mine. To make the trip, she went by way of the Manistee & North Eastern Railroad to Lake Ann, from there taking the horse-drawn stage which took her to Empire by a drive about twenty-five miles long. My mother was a heavy woman and none too well, so that this drive was a rather severe physical ordeal for her; and the expense of the trip was not too easily borne, for our family was decidedly poor. She had a very enjoyable time on the evening of her arrival; but at breakfast, about six o'clock the next morning, she said to my brother, "When does the stage go back to Lake Ann?" He told her that it left about seven o'clock. She told him to have the stage stop for her, as she must go back home. My brother, and my sister when she heard of it, protested very earnestly. Mother had come to spend a week with them: it was a trying drive and she ought not to go back under any circumstances so soon after coming out on the stage; everything was all right at home and there was no reason why she should go back. My mother told my brother and sister that she was needed at home, and that she must go back; and go back she did, though she could tell nothing as to the nature of the situation that called for her presence at home. Everything had been perfectly all right when she left on the previous morning.

What had actually happened was that my brother next younger than I had become ill during the night, and before morning the doctor had told us that he had pneumonia. From previous experiences of a somewhat similar nature, my father was so sure that my mother would know of our need and would be home that he went down to the train and met her when she came in on the evening train from Lake Ann, after driving from Empire to Lake Ann during the day (44, pp. 285-286; case 152 of Tabulation).

In answer to questions from Prince, Professor CN said that he was in his oldest brother's house at the time of his mother's impression and was thus a witness to her determination to go home. Prince sent Professor CN's statement to the oldest brother, asking him to make any correction which seemed appropriate. The brother replied that the statement was accurate in every respect.

The fourth illustrative case was reported by Ehrenwald in the A.S.P.R. *Journal*. The percipient was a patient of his, a married lady of forty named Lottie:

A native of Prague, she [Lottie] and her husband came to this country in 1938. Owing to circumstances beyond her control she was forced to leave her widowed mother, aged fifty-eight, behind in the country threatened by Nazi occupation. Lottie was torn with remorse for having done so, and she continued to do all in her power to obtain a visa for the old lady and to bring her over to the U.S.A. On April 12, 1939, between 10 and 10:30 A.M., Lottie was suddenly overcome by a feeling of anxiety and restlessness. She had a sense of some impending disaster and went into an uncontrollable crying fit. This happened in her apartment in New York. Helen, her maid, tried her best to calm her down and to find out the reason for Lottie's anxiety. But all Lottie could tell her was that she felt something terrible had happened to her mother, or maybe to her mother-in-law. Helen's consolation that she would not have to cry so bitterly if something had happened to her mother-in-law did not help matters. Lottie rushed to the phone and tried to put through a transatlantic telephone call to her mother. Owing to technical difficulties this was of no avail. She shared her anxiety with her husband and the next morning Lottie went to her safe deposit vault to parcel out what family heirlooms she had brought from the old country so that her mother, on her arrival here, would have an equal share of the jewels with her daughter—provided she would ever arrive. On her return from the bank Lottie's husband broke the news to her that in the night from April 12th to the 13th, her mother had suddenly passed away. The cable, sent by a relative, mentioned a carbuncle for which she had an operation. But Lottie learned a month or so later that her mother's death had been a suicide. On the critical night she had opened the gas jets in her apartment. Making allowance for the six hours' time difference between New York and Prague, Lottie's anxiety attack may have occurred after a latency period of several hours following her mother's mortal crisis. Like many cases of the kind there is, however, no information available as to the exact time she had succumbed to the gas poisoning (11, pp. 43-44; case 119 of Tabulation).

If cases of the impression type do include an element of extrasensory perception, they support the naturalness, and thus the genuineness, of more elaborate paranormal experiences which contain imagery, this on the grounds that since natural phenomena in general seem to manifest in grades of intensity and vividness, a similar grading should be expected of extrasensory perceptions as well. Also to be expected are similarities and even a blending with other "conventional" mental processes. Both these features are to be found in the examples presented in this monograph.

Impression cases also deserve study because they may add to our pitifully scanty knowledge of the processes of extrasensory perception. But first there must be reason to believe that they can contain an element of it. Although the conditions differ, the *principles* involved in deciding whether extrasensory perception is or is not present seem to be exactly the same for both spontaneous experiences and the results of laboratory investigations. Both depend on the assessment of probabilities as to whether or not the percipient could have inferred or had prior normal knowledge of the events which affected him at the time of his experience. Laboratory conditions have the advantage of permitting greater control over such sources of error as inference, lapses of memory, normal sensory communication, and so on. They also usually permit a firmer exclusion of chance in the evaluation of the data than is possible with most spontaneous cases. On the other hand, laboratory experiments have the disadvantage that the controls included in them seem liable to inhibit the emergence of extrasensory perception, at any rate in comparison with its apparently more frequent and richer appearance in ordinary life. Furthermore, laboratory experiments are by no means always convincing with regard to evidence of extrasensory perception. They also can have their flaws and among parapsychologists, as well as other scientists, an experiment considered adequately rigorous by one person may seem hopelessly loose to another. Thus, in the end, judgments about whether or not extrasensory perception did occur in a particular experiment depend upon a complex assessment of all sorts of factors, including how much confidence to place in the competence and integrity of both subjects and investigators. But this assessment of probabilities is exactly what is needed when judging spontaneous cases. They too rest on the integrity, accuracy of memory, and attention to detail of percipients, witnesses, and investigators.

I believe that adequate attention to relevant details can sometimes enable a spontaneous experience to be attributed with reasonable confidence to extrasensory perception. I also believe this to be true of simple impression experiences, even though these cannot, like cases which include imagery, be matched in several or many details with the related events (65, 67).

In my opinion an impression case may be considered to provide evidence for extrasensory perception when it satisfies the following criteria:

1. The percipient "feels" that the distant agent needs him, or is in some significant and unusual situation of which he has no normal knowledge at the time and no reason to infer or expect. Cases may be included in which the presumptive agent was not specifically identified, but the percipient had the impression that something was wrong "at home" or wherever the later identified agent then was.

2. The percipient's statement about the agent's need for him, or about the agent's situation, is also unusual. By "unusual," I mean that the percipient had never on other occasions expressed concern about the agent, or at any rate had never expressed it with such intensity and conviction, or so specifically, e.g., by saying that the agent had been in an accident, was in the hospital, or was dead. I have thus excluded instances of repeated gloomy forebodings which on one occasion happened to be right.

In some instances, of which I shall give examples later, the percipient makes no verbal statement, but simply acts to go toward the agent or otherwise help him.

3. The correspondence in time between impression and related event is close. This temporal coincidence is even more important in impression cases than in those with imagery, for along with identification of the agent, and the conviction that an important "something" is happening to him, it is one of the three available matching details between a simple impression and its related event. When a larger number of details are available for matching, as occur in most imaged perceptions, a more flexible attitude to correspondence in time may be allowed.

4. The report must satisfy adequate standards of authenticity, which should include independent corroboration for the fact that the percipient had his experience before he learned normally of the related events, about which there should also be independent verification.

A considerable number of impression cases conforming to these criteria have been published. If such cases are genuine they should show characteristics found also in other types of spontaneous cases. Moreover, if the older published cases were genuine, experiences of this kind must still be available for the further investigation which they deserve. This monograph therefore includes both a review of older published cases and the presentation of thirty-five previously unpublished cases.

The cases to be presented and analyzed will be offered in four sections. First, I shall present an analysis of 160 impression-type cases already published. Secondly, I shall present 23 (mostly) fairly recent, hitherto unpublished cases which have been rather thoroughly investigated and judged to be of relatively high authenticity. Thirdly, I shall present some examples of other types of cases related to the ordinary impression cases, such as cases without apparent agency and cases with physical symptoms apparently communicated. And finally, I shall discuss, with some additional illustrative cases, the contribution which these cases make to an understanding of the processes of extrasensory perception.

Chapter Two

REVIEW OF PREVIOUSLY PUBLISHED
IMPRESSION CASES

Method of Case Selection

Sources of Cases

Although a large number of impression cases has been published in different sources, many of them obviously lack authenticity[1] or have been reported with insufficient detail to permit judgment about authenticity and other features of importance in a systematic analysis of cases. I have therefore confined my search of the literature to the cases published by the Society for Psychical Research, the American Society for Psychical Research, the Boston Society for Psychic Research, and those published in *Phantasms of the Living* (18). This last work, although not an official publication of the S.P.R., was compiled by three of its early leaders using standards of authenticity similar to those set by the Society. Many of the cases in *Phantasms* were also published in the *Journal* or *Proceedings* of the S.P.R. and later in F. W. H. Myers' *Human Personality and its Survival of Bodily Death* (37).

I made (with the help of L. A. Dale) a systematic search for every impression case published in the above four sources. The

---

[1] By "authenticity" I mean a close correspondence between the published reports and the events they are claimed to describe. A map is authentic if the cities, rivers, and mountains it represents have distances from one another on it that are proportional to the distances between these places actually measured; and I think a case report can in a similar way be judged to be a more or less authentic representation of the events it purports to describe.

search of the publications of the Societies was taken up to the end of 1967.

Criteria for Inclusion of Cases in Analysis

For the present analysis I accepted all impression cases I could find in the above sources *except* the following:

1. Cases in which the percipient's apparently paranormal knowledge referred to a future or a definitely passed (as opposed to a contemporaneous) event. (A case was included if the impression occurred not more than twenty-four hours after the death of the presumed agent.)

2. Cases in which the agent's difficulty was not sharply limited in time as well as specific in nature. Thus, awareness by the percipient that the agent had a vague illness which extended over some weeks would not be included.

3. Cases without any possible living human agent, e.g., instances of apparently clairvoyant impressions or instances in which an animal might have acted as the agent, or in which a long-deceased human being was the ostensible agent. (But, as mentioned above, cases with dying or just recently deceased agents were included.)

4. Cases in which the *main* feature of the experience was some form of sensory imagery, although in a few of the included cases some sensory imagery formed a subsidiary part of the experience.

5. Cases in which, from my review of the data presented, I concluded that some subjective factor, rational inference, or normal means of communication might sufficiently account for the experience reported.

6. Cases reported with insufficient detail to permit judgment about any of the above features. (I have also excluded a few cases in which scanty detail precluded the case from being useful in a full analysis of factors under study in this monograph.)

When more than one impression experience was attributed to a percipient, I included only one of the several reported experiences attributed to him. This seemed best for studying patterns of relationships between percipients and agents.

The rejection of a number of cases for the above reasons led finally to the inclusion in the analysis of the following number of cases:

	Number of Cases
Journal of the A.S.P.R.	29
Proceedings and *Journal* of the S.P.R.	61
Phantasms of the Living	34
Bulletin of the Boston S.P.R.	36
Total	160

The majority (although by no means all) of the included cases have corroborations independent of the percipient and a large number are reported with the results of additional investigation by responsible authors or editors. They thus comprise the best authenticated examples of impression cases so far published in the English language. The Tabulation given above provides the reader with a full list of the included cases. In nearly every instance I have given the *first* publication of a report if it was published in more than one place. Many cases published in the first volumes of the *Proceedings* and *Journal* of the S.P.R. were also included in *Phantasms of the Living* and some were reprinted in later analyses of series, e.g., by Sidgwick (61). In a few instances I have cited a publication later than the first when the later publication included more detail, an additional corroboration, etc. The Tabulation also indicates the principal features of the cases that have entered into the following analysis.

ANALYSIS OF PUBLISHED CASES

In the following analysis of these 160 cases, as well as in presenting new cases and in discussing all cases, I shall use the term "agent" for the person about whom the percipient obtains information. (Such a person is sometimes better referred to as the "target person.") This use of the word "agent," however, does not imply that the person concerned was necessarily the active source of the information communicated to the percipient. As the case reports will show, a person other than the target person may have been (or sometimes thought that he was) the active sender of a call for help to the percipient. In some cases it is possible to assign two or more persons to the role of agent in this sense.

Table 2 gives the number of percipients and agents of each sex. There were 84 female and 76 male percipients. There were 62 female agents and 98 male agents. Agent and percipient were of the same sex in 74 cases, of different sexes in 86 cases.

Table 2

SEX OF PERCIPIENTS AND AGENTS

	Female	*Male*	*Total*
Sex of Percipient	84 (52.5%)	76 (47.5%)	160
Sex of Agent	62 (39.0%)	98 (61.0%)	160

Note: The sex of the presumed agent was occasionally doubtful since in a few cases more than one person could have filled the role of agent. This could happen especially when both an adult and an attended infant or child were in distress.

It is noteworthy that in some other series of spontaneous cases females showed a marked preponderance over males as percipients. For example, the ratio of female to male percipients was 4 to 1 in the 1960 S.P.R. series (17) and 2.3 to 1 in the German series published by Sannwald (56, 57). Both these series included some impression cases in their totals, but also other types of spontaneous cases. Such marked preponderance of female percipients may arise from a greater tendency on the part of women to report apparently paranormal experiences to investigators or during surveys. The present series, however, does not show such a large preponderance of female percipients. Nor did the *Phantasms of the Living* series in which 58 per cent of the percipients were females and 42 per cent males (18). And in the Indian series, which did not depend on voluntary submission of reports by the percipients, almost equal percentages of boys (35.8 per cent) and girls (36.8 per cent) among the children answering the questionnaire of the survey reported that they had had one or more experiences of extrasensory perception (41).

The present series shows a marked preponderance of male agents. Male agents also preponderated in the *Phantasms of the Living* series where they were 63 per cent of the total (18) and in the 1960 S.P.R. series where they were 64 per cent of the total (17). The marked preponderance of male agents in the present series suggests, having regard to the actually greater proportion of female percipients, that in these experiences women have a greater tendency than men to be in touch paranormally with members of the opposite sex.

Relationship Between Percipient and Agent
    Table 3 gives the data of the relationship between the per-

Table 3

RELATIONSHIP OF PERCIPIENTS AND AGENTS

1. Members of Same Immediate Family		
Husband-Wife	22 (13.7%)	
Siblings	24 (15.0%)	
Parent-Child	54 (33.8%)	
Subtotal:		100 (62.5%)
2. Members of Extended Family (Cousins, In-laws, Grandparents, etc.)	11 (6.9%)	
3. Friends and Acquaintances	45 (28.1%)	
4. Strangers	4 (2.5%)	
Subtotal:		60 (37.5%)
Total:		160

cipients and the presumptive agents in these cases. As in most similar analyses (17, 41, 56, 57), immediate family relationships preponderate.[2] The difference between sibling combinations and

---

[2] The proportion of family relationships between percipient and agent was considerably lower in the *Phantasms of the Living* series. In that series only (roughly) 47 per cent of the percipients had some blood relationship to the agent, in 6 per cent they were husband and wife, and in 47 per cent friends, acquaintances or strangers (18).

parent-child combinations is probably not significant since in each family with at least one child there are three persons who may enter into parent-child combinations.

The series contains very few strangers as agents. This feature accords with observations of most other series of spontaneous cases in which strangers are rarely involved as presumptive agents (17, 18, 41, 56, 57). The small *Titanic* series of nineteen cases forms an exception to this trend (64, 66).

It has been argued that the paucity of stranger agents in spontaneous cases arises from the difficulty of verifying perceptions when the persons concerned do not know each other. Percipients will also tend to remember and report those experiences which are verified and so we may have a spurious preponderance of agents among the members of the immediate families of the percipients. This may be part of the story, but it is unlikely to be the whole of it. It is almost as easy to verify a perception with friends and acquaintances and with more distant relatives as with members of one's immediate family. And yet in the present analyses as well as others cited, we find a marked preponderance of immediate family relationships between the percipients and agents. I interpret this as additional evidence of the role of emotional factors in the processes of extrasensory perception.

The relatively high proportion of marital partners, friends and acquaintances, and strangers in the agent-percipient relationships (together comprising 50 per cent of the total) gives no support to the idea that *biological* relationships facilitate extrasensory perception. Emotional ties seem to be more important than biological ones. It happens that we have most opportunity for developing emotional ties with persons with whom we initially have biological relationships. But such emotional ties develop through shared experiences and not from biological relationships as such.

Situation of Agent at Time of Experience

Table 4 gives a breakdown of the situation of the agent in this series and in four other series into three major categories: "Death (or Dying)," "Important (or Dangerous)," and "Not Serious (or Not Dangerous)." I believe that the other series of sponta-

Table 4

SITUATION OF AGENT AT TIME OF EXPERIENCE IN IMPRESSION CASES AND OTHER TYPES OF SPONTANEOUS CASES OF SEVERAL SERIES (PERCENTAGES ONLY)

	Present Series (Impression Cases Only)	Saltmarsh Series[1]	English Series[2]	German Series[3]	Indian Series[4]
Death (or Dying)	41.0%	34.5%	28.3%	43.1%	46.3%
Important (or Dangerous) (Serious illness, accident, near drowning, etc.)	41.0%	30.3%	24.3%	36.4%	29.7%
Not Serious (or not Dangerous)	18.0%	Not Included as a Category	Data Not Comparable	17.7%	4.5%
Trivial	0	35.2%	Data Not Comparable	2.8%	0
Miscellaneous (Not otherwise classified)	0	0	0	0	19.5%

[1] Taken from Ref. 55, Table and text on pp. 54-55. This series contains only precognitive cases.

[2] Taken from Ref. 17, Figures 24 and 27, pp. 136 and 138. Since all the impression cases in the present series were related to contemporaneous events, the cases in the English (S.P.R.) series related to *past* deaths are not included; but the English series does contain some precognitive cases not separately identified in the tables of the S.P.R. report. (Two impression cases in this English series are also included in the present series given in Column 2.)

[3] Taken from Ref. 57.

[4] Taken from Ref. 41.

neous cases (17, 41, 55, 56, 57) contain data which can be compared with those of the present series. To permit such a comparison I have combined certain categories which are separate in the tables of the other reports, but readers should consult the original reports to assure themselves that my comparisons are justified.

Death is a fairly well defined event, although in some cases of this series it has not been possible to ascertain whether the presumptive agent was dying or actually dead at the time of the experience. I have made an arbitrary division between Important or Dangerous and Not Serious or Not Dangerous situations. Under the heading "Important" are classified situations carrying a threat to life, e.g., a serious illness, shipwreck with danger of drowning, severe accidents, etc. The phrase "Not Serious or not Dangerous" seems preferable to the term "trivial," which is often used, for it emphasizes that the agent's situation may not have seemed trivial to him, even though it caused him only minor inconvenience and was certainly not dangerous. The present series includes few cases in which the word "trivial" would seem apposite; as in other series of spontaneous cases, it shows a high incidence of situations of danger or death for the presumptive agent.

The rarity of trivial situations in impression cases deserves some further comment. It may arise simply from the lack of detail which in imaged impressions may lead to verification of extrasensory perceptions related to trivial events. Or it may be that a special intensity of emotion is required to penetrate consciousness in the form of an impression experience since this is largely one of feeling rather than of cognition. Such emotion would be less likely to be generated in trivial situations. In the report of the 1960 S.P.R. series Green comments as follows:

> Cases of threatened danger contained the highest percentage of "intuitions" [corresponding to impression cases], 36.8 per cent. As these cases could perhaps be regarded as the most urgent type of all, it could be that the subconscious mind had no time to elaborate the impression received into an hallucination or a dream, or that their special urgency enabled them to penetrate the consciousness of persons not liable to hallucinatory impressions (17, p. 113).

Unfortunately, the report of the 1960 S.P.R. series does not give the percentage of impression or intuitive experiences which related to threatened danger or other serious situations, nor does there seem to be any way of comparing such cases in the S.P.R. report with the categories in the present series. But there is a suggestion in the data of both series that impression experiences have a higher percentage of serious situations as their themes than have hallucinatory experiences. In addition, a further analysis of the present series shows a high proportion of unexpected situations among the circumstances of the agents. Table 5 gives a further breakdown of the agents' situations for these 160 cases.

Table 5

Details of Agent's Circumstances at Time of Experience

Dying

Death from natural causes, but in the course of a progressive illness	15		
Death from natural causes but sudden; agent apparently in good health but dies within a few days, often within a few hours, of becoming ill	22		
Violent or accidental death (automobile and airplane accidents, homicide, suicide, etc.)	15		
Total for which causes of death adequately recorded		52	
Total for which causes of death not adequately recorded		14	
Total deaths:			66

Serious

In accident	17		
In danger of drowning	4		
In danger from fire	5		
Total serious accidents		26	
Total other causes for serious situation of agent		41	
Total all cases in which agent is judged to be in serious situation			67
Not Serious			27
Total all cases:			160

From Table 5 it can be seen that in 37 cases with the agent dying, his death was quite sudden and occurred either from violence or accident; or, if occurring from natural causes, it took place within a few hours or (at most) a few days of his being in apparent good health. I do not know of any data from a normal population showing the expectation of death from a brief illness as compared with a long one, but I have the distinct impression that death from prolonged illness is much commoner in the general population than it is in the present series, which contains a high proportion of sudden, quite unexpected deaths among those agents dying of natural causes. The reports frequently state that the agent "dropped dead" or went to bed apparently healthy and was found dead the next morning.

Violent deaths amount to almost a third (29 per cent) of the total number of deaths with recorded causes in this series. In 1966 deaths from accidents, suicide, and homicide combined accounted for only 7.7 per cent of all deaths in the United States (77), so that the incidence of such violent deaths in the present series is almost four times the expected incidence. The vital statistics of the United States for 1966 would provide a conservative figure for comparison since deaths from violent causes have been increasing in the United States and would have been markedly less throughout the period when most of these cases occurred. Also the fact that more than half the cases analyzed were British cases would only make the comparison more marked between the incidence of violent deaths in this series and in the general population. Violent deaths (accidents, homicide, and suicide) made up only 4.3 per cent of all deaths in England and Wales in 1966 (9).

It may be argued that the cases of this series have been selected to exclude agents with prolonged illnesses whose conditions would be normally known to the percipients. This point, however, is taken care of in the acceptance of the cases for publication since the percipient in all cases, even if he knew that the agent was ill, did not have any expectation that he would die. We are concerned here, then, not with the percipient's expectation of the agent's death, but with the agent's expectation of his own death.

We find also a high incidence of unexpected events among

the agents' circumstances characterized as "serious." Serious accidents account for more than a third of the cases in which the agent, although not dying, was in a dangerous situation and needing help.

These data suggest that the suddenness of the change in the agent's circumstances, generating perhaps an intenser emotion than occurs in tragedies seen in advance, may have been a factor in "agency power" and hence in the stimulation of the percipient's experience. I should add, however, that such unexpectedness of the agent's situation is not confined to impression cases. I found it also in a series of 125 precognitive dreams (69).

Very few of the agents in the 160 cases of the present series communicated or sought to communicate "good news." Among the 27 "Not Serious" events there were ten "arrivals" communicated and one proposal of marriage. In nearly all the other cases of this subgroup the agent was in some kind of trouble and requiring help. It may seem that the high incidence in the agents' situations of life-threatening or other serious events is due to the greater memorableness of such events. But, as West has pointed out (81, p. 200), many pleasant events such as births, marriages, and business successes are just as memorable as unpleasant ones and yet they do not figure in spontaneous cases nearly so frequently as do the unpleasant events. The marked difference suggests that the need for help on the part of the agent plays an important part in the processes of the experience.

Circumstances of Percipient at Time of Impression

Table 6 gives a breakdown of the data with regard to the state of consciousness and the social situation of the percipient at the time of the impression. It can be seen that most of the percipients about whom there is information on these points were awake and about half of them were with other people when their impressions occurred.

West has expressed the view that "spontaneous impressions most commonly come when the person is alone and relaxed. It is unusual for someone who is in company, with his attention absorbed, to be interrupted by a psychic impression" (80, p. 40).

Table 6

CIRCUMSTANCES OF PERCIPIENT AT TIME OF IMPRESSION

(a) State of Consciousness		
Awake	143 (89.4%)	
Asleep	17 (10.6%)	
Total:		160
(b) Social Situation		
Alone	54 (33.7%)	
With Others	71 (44.4%)	
Unknown	35 (21.9%)	
Total:		160

Note: Percipients who were asleep were arbitrarily considered to be alone, even though someone else might be in the same room with them.

The apparent discrepancy between the data of this series and West's opinion may lie in the key words, "with his attention absorbed." One can be passive in company, and even daydream when being dummy at bridge. There is no reason to suppose that the presence of other people facilitates extrasensory perception, but it does not necessarily interfere with it (although, as I shall show later, it may tend to reduce the emergence of more detail in the perceptions).

Action Taken by Percipient

As shown in Table 7, in 83 (52 per cent) of the 160 cases the percipient's impression drove him to take some kind of action apart from merely telling other people about it or making a written record. The most frequent action was to make some move toward the identified agent such as going to him or to his home, or sending him a letter or telegram. In some instances judgment about whether what the percipient did amounted to "action" became difficult. In one case a woman who was depressed and weeping got into a cab and had herself driven around the city, rather aimlessly as it happened, since she had not localized the agent (her husband) related to her distress. This was counted as "action." When the percipient simply requested other people to remain with him during his discomfort I did not count this behavior as "action," although if the percipient went to other people for comfort or reassurance in his distress, I did count it as such. In a few cases, the percipient felt moved to pray for the agent and I counted this as "action."

In their efforts to reach the agents, the percipients frequently ignored all rational considerations. They often changed plans abruptly, broke off holidays, traveled many miles in discomfort, and put up with or imposed on other persons all kinds of inconveniences in order to get to the places where they felt they should be. They generally disregarded all interfering or cautionary suggestions from bystanders. To onlookers they might have seemed almost ruthless in their determination to reach the agent, but they remained oblivious of such reproaches.

The taking of action is an objective or behavioristic criterion of conviction about an impression. Other percipients may have had a sense of conviction without acting upon it, and further information might well have disclosed that many more than 52 per cent of the percipients had it. In L. E. Rhine's series of 1,839 waking intuitive (impression) cases she found that 84 per cent of

Table 7

CASES IN WHICH PERCIPIENT TOOK ACTION
BASED ON HIS IMPRESSION

	All Cases	With Reference to Agent Focusing on Percipient		With Reference to Percipient's Identification of Agent	
		Agent Focusing	Agent Not Focusing[1]	Agent Identified	Agent Not Identified
Action Taken by Percipient	83 (52%)	32* (69%)	51* (45%)	54 (51%)	29 (53%)
Action Not Taken by Percipient	77 (48%)	14 (31%)	63 (55%)	50 (49%)	27 (47%)
Total:	160 (100%)	46 (100%)	114 (100%)	104 (100%)	56 (100%)

[1] Category of "Agent Not Focusing (on Percipient)" includes cases in which there is no information on this point one way or the other. It is therefore possible that more agents were focusing on the percipient than are known to have done so from the reports.
* Chi-square test of the significance of the difference between the asterisked figures gives P<.01.

the percipients had a sense of conviction (49); but, in contrast, Green reported only 17 percipients (37 per cent) in 46 cases of the intuitive type as having it (17). This incidence is far lower than that of the present series and Rhine's.

In 56 cases of the present series, the percipient did not identify a specific person as being in distress. In 27 (53 per cent) of these 56 cases, the percipient nevertheless took action such as going, telephoning, or telegraphing home (see Table 7). One percipient (already mentioned) just got a cab and had herself driven around the town, but the others (with rare exceptions) did something more definite toward verifying the impression or succoring whomever might be in trouble, for example, at home. These cases of usually appropriate action taken without any identification of a particular person being in trouble or of the nature of that trouble show in the purest form the power, so it seems to me, of extrasensory perception to influence behavior while the provenance and process of the influence remain completely unconscious. In cases such as these, the percipient is only aware of intense feelings and impulses toward action, but still he acts on the basis of these alone. The behavior of some of the percipients as they described it themselves reminds one of marionettes controlled by a puppeteer, or of a subject responding to a posthypnotic suggestion while showing complete amnesia for the implanted suggestion which is in fact the origin of the irresistible impulse to his action.

A further point emerges from an analysis of the cases in which the percipient took action in relation to those cases in which the agent consciously focused on the percipient.[3] As already mentioned, 52 per cent of all the percipients did act on their impressions. In 46 cases, the agent was focusing attention on the percipient and in 32 (69 per cent) of such cases the percipients took action. In contrast, the percipients took action in only 45 per cent of the cases with agent not focusing. The difference between these two figures is significant with $P < .01$ (see Table 7). This difference

---

[3] What I refer to as "agent focusing on the percipient" includes a rather wide range of thoughts from, at one extreme, a simple thought of the percipient on the part of the agent to, at the other extreme, intense and sometimes vocalized pleas for help consciously directed toward the percipient. The quality and intensity of such "agent focusing" needs much more study.

suggests that the conscious focusing of the agent on the percipient increased the "power" of the communicated extrasensory impression, or at least of its emotional and impulse-generating components.

Agent focusing was a more important factor in percipient action than was the seriousness of the agent's physical condition because among the 66 cases in which the agent was dying the percipient took action in only 29, a proportion (44 per cent) below that for the series as a whole in which 52 per cent of the percipients took action.

Emotions Felt by Percipient

Many of the reports of these cases do not mention the percipient's emotion at the time of his experience. This may be due to inadequate reporting and investigation, or it may be due to a tendency for the impulse to action to suppress or at least diminish felt emotions in the percipient.

When an emotion is reported for the percipient, it is in nearly every case one of either anxiety or depression or both. Only a handful of the percipients experienced pleasurable emotions and these were nearly all found in the "Not Serious" cases. One percipient, however, reported "joy" in relation to the impression of the death of a sister.

As already mentioned, the presumptive agent was dying or had just died in 66 cases. In 36 of these cases we have reasonably precise reports of the percipient's emotional or physical state during his experience; in the remaining 30 cases the percipient's feelings were not stated or were given imprecisely. Table 8 gives a breakdown of the data for these 66 Death cases.

In the 36 cases for which information on this point is available, the percipient showed depression in 13 instances, anxiety in 22 instances, and joy in one. One percipient showed both depression and anxiety, but was included once only under anxiety. Either of these emotions could be considered appropriate during the experience or expectation of losing a loved relative or friend.

Some of the percipients became, according to the reports, markedly depressed and one committed suicide on the basis of a correct impression of his father's death miles away.

Table 8

EMOTIONAL CONDITION OF PERCIPIENT IN 66 IMPRESSION
CASES WITH AGENT DYING

	Anxiety	Depression	Joy	Not Stated or Given Imprecisely
With Agent Identified	9	4	0	19
With Agent Not Identified	13	9	1	11
Total:	22	13	1	30

Note: One percipient was reported as being both depressed and anxious and was included once here under Anxiety. If a percipient was reported as weeping without other characterization of the emotion, he was included under Depression.

Twenty-two of the percipients did not identify the dying or deceased agent and yet nevertheless included a response of either anxiety or depression in their experiences. They thus showed the appropriate emotion to the loss without identifying the person they had lost. In a considerable number of these cases the percipient took no action, or no impulse to action was reported. Thus the experience consisted exclusively of an unexpected, rather sudden change of emotion. Some percipients burst into tears, or trembled, or yielded to a strong desire to pray. In such cases the evidence for a paranormal process is naturally slighter than in cases in which the percipient correctly localizes the agent, or at least the site of trouble. Nevertheless, the percipient (and sometimes the corroborators) testifies that the mood change which came over him was unusual and unexpected.

Cases of this type with change of emotions only have an important bearing on the broader question of how much people may influence each other's moods through extrasensory processes.

Physical Symptoms Occurring During Experience

Fourteen percipients had definite physical symptoms during the impression experience. Four of these felt so ill or weak that they thought they themselves were going to die. One percipient developed jaundice. Four percipients experienced pain and in two of these pain cases the agent was having labor pains at the time of the experience.

Additional Details in the Impression

Fifty-eight of the 160 percipients stated details of the agent's situation additional to the information (usually given) that he was in distress. The additional information included such items as that the agent had died or had been in an accident.

The social situation of the percipient was not correlated with additional details in the impression, because 24 of the percipients obtaining additional details were alone at the time of the experience, 23 were with other persons and in 11 cases the report does not give information about the percipient's social situation.

The seriousness of the agent's physical condition also did not correlate with the occurrence of additional details in the impression. There were only 21 cases with the agent dying among the 58 cases with additional details, a proportion (36 per cent) of "dying cases" less than that for the series as a whole, which was 42 per cent.

Additional details in the impression were correlated negatively with action on the part of the percipient. Thus 83 (52 per cent) of all 160 percipients took action (see Table 7), but of the 58 percipients having additional details in their experiences only 22 (38 per cent) took action. The taking of action may have blocked the emergence of more details in some of the impressions.

Additional details in the impression were also not correlated with agent focusing on the percipient. Agent focusing on the percipient was reported to have occurred in only 15 (26 per cent) of the impressions with additional details. In the whole group of 160 cases, 46 (28 per cent) of the agents were reported to have focused on the percipient. There was, however, a suggestion that when the agent focused on the percipient the latter was more likely to identify the agent than when he did not. Thus among 46 cases with agent focusing, the percipient identified the agent in 32 (70 per cent) whereas among 114 cases with the agent not focusing, the percipient identified him in 71 (63 per cent).

Concluding Remarks About Previously Published Cases

The foregoing analysis has brought out several features of these impression cases that I shall briefly summarize.

1. Impression cases were found to show resemblances in their characteristics to other kinds of spontaneous cases as, for example, in the high incidence of death and serious situations in the circumstances of the agent, and in the frequent occurrence of close emotional ties between agent and percipient. These similarities of characteristics provide further evidence of the authenticity of the cases, additional to the individual investigations they received before publication. They suggest that spontaneous cases, including impression cases, belong to naturally occurring types of experience. These recurrent patterns, however, do not by themselves increase the evidence for paranormal processes in the cases.

2. Agent focusing was positively correlated with action taken by the percipient in response to his experience, but seriousness of the agent's situation as indicated by his dying was not correlated with action on the part of the percipient.

3. Impression cases show a variety of forms. On the one hand, they may include details additional to the bare impression of someone in distress. And on the other hand, they may consist only of a pure emotion or of some impulsive action. Such emotion or action on the part of the percipient may occur without his having identified the agent as the person in distress and the presumptive stimulus of his response. Nevertheless, the percipient's emotion or action may be appropriate to the situation, e.g., death of the agent.

Chapter Three

TWENTY-THREE NEW IMPRESSION CASES

INTRODUCTORY REMARKS

The following cases have all been investigated rather thoroughly by myself.[1] All but four of them have clear corroboration that the percipient told or recorded his impression before he had normal knowledge of the related events. (In one of the four exceptions the percipient took unusual action to find her husband in the middle of the night and he corroborated this.) All but one also include some independent evidence verifying the related events. In twenty-one of the cases I have had interviews with the percipients and/or one or more other main informants. Investigation of the remaining two cases was conducted by correspondence alone.

All the cases in this group of twenty-three satisfy the criteria of a percipient making an unusual statement (or carrying out an unusual action) with regard to someone at a distance who was in distress or dying and whose condition was not normally known to the percipient or one that he could have inferred from available facts.

---

[1] I am interested in hearing of additional cases suggestive of extrasensory perception whether of the impression type or of any other type. Informants should, however, be prepared to enter into correspondence and, when feasible, interviews, concerning details. And they should be willing to permit publication of their experiences, with pseudonyms if desired.

CASE REPORTS

Case 1[2]

The testimony in this case comes from the percipient, Mrs. Rose Rudkin,[3] and her son, Thaddeus Rudkin, from whom I first heard of it in a conversation (in Miami, Florida) in the autumn of 1961. At my request, Mr. Rudkin asked his mother to write an account of her experience, and he too recorded independently his own recollection of the event. Some subsequent correspondence ensued about details. Mrs. Rudkin's original testimony was sent to me in a letter[4] dated December 3, 1961, as follows:

> In 1930 I was living in London, England. My mother, aged 75, had not been well and was living in Cleveland, Ohio. On January 9th I awoke in the morning knowing that my mother had died during the night and I so informed my family at the breakfast table. They wanted to know if I had heard from home. Then I said I had not, but I knew with certainty that she had died. Before we had finished our breakfast a cablegram was delivered telling us of her death. I do not know why I was so sure. I only know that when I woke up that morning I was convinced that my mother had died during the night.

Mr. Rudkin's testimony is dated January 2, 1962.

> I have a vivid recollection of the episode which I related to you involving my mother's awareness of her mother's death prior to learning of it through ordinary methods of human communication. At the time, my maternal grandmother was approximately 75 years of age and lived in Cleveland, Ohio. She

---

2 All previously unpublished cases in this monograph are given a consecutive case number.

3 Pseudonym. Seven of the new cases in this monograph have been reported with pseudonyms for the percipient, agent, and other informants. I have used pseudonyms for some persons and places mentioned in Mrs. Hellström's cases (Cases 16 to 21). For all other cases, however, I have been asked or given permission to use real names and have done so.

4 In reproducing written statements by percipients and other informants I have occasionally made minor editorial corrections of grammar or punctuation to permit easier reading and I have interpolated a few explanatory remarks. When I have omitted words I have indicated this by ellipses and when I have inserted words they have been placed in brackets.

had been widowed for many years and lived with her bachelor sons. My impression is that she was not in good health and did suffer from the ailments connected with old age. My impression also is that whatever her condition was, it was not different than it had been for some months. I had a great affection for my grandmother and frequently stayed with her when her sons were out of town and when she otherwise would have been alone.

At the time of the incident, I had not seen her for about three or four years since we had lived in London, England, throughout that period while she remained in Cleveland, Ohio. On the morning in question, I remember being downstairs when mother came down for breakfast. She was weeping. This was quite unusual in my experience because my mother has always been a somewhat stoical person and not usually given to tears. I asked her why she was crying and she said quite simply: "Mother died last night." I said, "How do you know that she died?" I would have been aware of a phone call if there had been one, or if there had been any mail that morning. At that time, I could get no further reply from her than, "I just know she died last night." The time of this incident would have been about 8 o'clock in the morning. Later that morning, mother received a cablegram from her brother advising her of grandma's death that night.

I have not consulted my mother to see whether my recollection is the same as hers. I am, however, sending her a copy of this letter and if she has a different recollection of events, she will undoubtedly communicate with you.

(Mrs. Rudkin had, in fact, already written her account at the time Mr. Rudkin wrote his.)

I then asked Mr. Rudkin whether the time of his grandmother's death could be confirmed independently, and also to what extent his story and his mother's were independent. Mr. Rudkin replied on January 17, 1962:

"The account I gave you was as I remembered the incident. I do not recall ever discussing it with my mother, although it is entirely possible that I did so over the years. I have told the story many times over the years, but I am quite positive that my recollection is an independent one.

In an effort to pin down the exact time of grandma's death, I have obtained a copy of the death certificate filed by the attending physician. This shows that death occurred on January 8, 1930, at 11:00 A.M. The time of death in London would have been at approximately 4:00 P.M. on the 8th. My first recollection of the matter is, of course, at breakfast time on the 9th. Mother became aware of her mother's death sometime after she retired on the night of the 8th and prior to breakfast on the 9th. It is therefore clear that whatever mother's experience was, it took place hours after her mother's death.

I had also written to Mrs. Rudkin asking how much she had already known about her mother's condition before her experience, and also for further details of it. She replied on January 3, 1962:

In answer to your letter of December 28th I wish to advise that I had no knowledge that my mother was seriously ill. I knew she had been bothered with rheumatism.

I awakened on the morning of January 9th, 1930, with a very strong feeling that my mother had died. It was only a general impression and did not include any image of a visual or auditory kind. A cable was delivered about one hour after I awoke saying my mother had died the night before.

Subsequently, on January 29, 1962, Mrs. Rudkin forwarded me a photostat copy of her mother's death certificate, which gave the time of death (in Cleveland, Ohio) as 11:00 A.M. January 8, 1930. This would have been 4:00 P.M. London time.

The time of death being thus established, it is clear that the percipient was wrong in stating that her mother had died "the night before" she told her family of her conviction and Mr. Rudkin was wrong also in stating that the cablegram had given the time of death as "that night." In a letter to me of February 14, 1969, Mr. Rudkin acknowledged the discrepancies and said they were probably due to the fact that his uncle, who was then in the United States and learned first of the death of the percipient's mother, had the habit of sending "night letters" that would be dispatched at night and arrive the next morning. The percipient became aware of her mother's death after a period of latency and she very naturally thought her impression coincided with the time of death more closely than it did. Mr. Rudkin made the understandable slip of assuming that the cable arrived just a few hours after the death of the agent.

In reply to a question as to whether Mrs. Rudkin was in the habit of having forebodings of misfortune or death, Mr. Rudkin wrote me on April 25, 1964, as follows:

> Specifically in reply to your inquiry, I am quite sure that this was a unique experience so far as mother is concerned. She never reported any earlier experience of believing that her mother was dead or dying. Mother is a cheerful person by nature, not inclined to the morbid side of things.

As regards possible motivation in this case, it may be worth mentioning that, as a young woman, Mrs. Rudkin's mother had had an auditory hallucination of her own mother's voice calling her name, which she said coincided in time with her mother's death. Mrs. Rudkin, as a child, heard her mother describe this experience immediately after it happened, which suggests that when the time came for her mother to die, her mother may have tried to communicate with her (Mrs. Rudkin) as she (Mrs. Rudkin's mother) believed her mother had done with her.

It is worth noting here that Mrs. Rudkin's impression did not emerge until she was asleep, presumably between about six and fourteen hours after her mother's actual death. The case thus belongs to the small group of impression cases in which the percipient was asleep at the time of the impression (see Table 6, p. 23).

Case 2

Miss Alice Langley (pseudonym) of Long Beach, California, who has herself had a number of experiences suggestive of extrasensory perception, sent me the following case in which she was the agent in a letter dated March 18, 1962. (Subsequently I had an interview with Miss Langley at Long Beach, California, during which we discussed details of this case and others in which she was the percipient.) The relevant portions of her letter follow:

I used to wonder if I could "send" as well as I could receive, telepathically. Then in 1956, my parents along with my mother's older cousin (a woman) went up to the San Joaquin Valley to attend the funeral of their 88-year-old uncle. This was about 300 miles distant. I was working at the college then [in Long Beach, California] and didn't mind being left alone. That is, not until the third evening. I was sitting in the dimness of the living room, watching television without any lights on, when someone came to the door and began pounding vigorously upon it. It was my mother's youngest brother, a veritable black sheep of the family, and he was loudly drunk.

It seems that he had been on a fishing trip and was bringing my mother a tuna. I'm terrified of drunks, so naturally, I didn't let him in. But he wouldn't take my word that my mother wasn't at home. He just kept pounding and yelling. Admittedly I was in a panic. I sat on the floor in front of the television, not knowing quite what to do. Then with all the power I could muster, I sent a frantic S.O.S. to my folks—just *"Please Come Home!"* I glanced at the clock. It was 8:20 P.M. I knew, of course, that they couldn't possibly get home in time to help me out of that situation, but my sense of security was shattered. I phoned the police. They arrived rather promptly, and promised to keep a protective eye on our house, but my uncle had disappeared. He left his car out in front, however, so he might have returned at any time. I was still glad I'd sent that S.O.S., though, because I didn't want to spend another night alone after that.

The next day my thoughts were strongly on my folks' return. There had been no pre-arrangements as to when they were coming back, because we've a lot of relatives in the town where they were visiting and I knew that they were undoubtedly having a good visit. But at 2:10 P.M. [at work] my feeling that they must surely have returned was so keen that I phoned home. My timing was nothing short of perfect—they were just walking in the door when the phone rang. And it was my first call, too.

Later that day, when my mother and I compared notes, I learned that she had felt perfectly at ease about me until suddenly, on the evening in question, she'd had a sudden feeling that I needed her. She mentioned it to her cousin and she, too, felt it. They looked at the clock and found that it was 8:20 P.M. My dad didn't get the message at all.

In reply to my request for corroboration, if possible, from her mother and other witnesses, Miss Langley wrote that her stepfather and her mother's cousin had died since 1956; but she enclosed a statement, signed by her mother, Mrs. Rebecca Langley, who had dictated it because she was ill at the time. Both Miss Langley's letter and the statement were dated April 28, 1962. The statement follows:

> On the evening of September 4, 1956, I was visiting relatives in the city of Visalia, California, following the funeral of my uncle. My husband and my cousin had made the trip up there with me from Long Beach. We were having a nice visit with our relatives when about 8:20 P.M. I got a sudden urge that I should go home. I felt uneasy concerning my daughter being home alone, and I spoke to my cousin and husband about it. And we decided to leave early next morning.
>
> My cousin said that she felt that way too. Our relations begged us to stay longer, but I could hardly wait until I got home. We left early the next day and drove down by car.
>
> When we arrived home, I could hear the phone ringing while I was unlocking the door. When I answered, it was my daughter and she told me what a scare she got the previous evening. When I asked her what time it happened, she told me it was about 8:20 P.M. When she got home from college that day, we talked it over and decided it was exactly the same time as she had sent me the mental telepathy message.
>
> It never seemed to affect my husband, but my cousin felt it. I lost my cousin just this past March 3rd.

Later I wrote asking Miss Langley if her mother had any tendency to break off trips irrationally, and she replied in a letter dated February 22, 1964:

> . . . I'll begin by answering your question as to whether or not my mother had upon other occasions returned unexpectedly from trips.
>
> No. As a matter of fact, she was not in the habit of taking trips other than those we undertook as a family. The only other incident comparable to the one to which you refer was the time

she and I both persuaded my dad to cut short our motor vacation because we both (Mother and myself) had an unaccountable sense of urgency to get home quickly. After much grumbling, my dad gave in and brought us home. We were each a little disappointed that there seemed to be no reason for our apprehension. But—two days later, I was taken to the hospital for an emergency operation, and my physician told me that it was only by the greatest luck that we had returned as we did, since I wouldn't have survived if I hadn't received prompt medical attention.

Case 3

Mr. Richard Sternberg (pseudonym) first told me about this case verbally, and it was afterwards confirmed in writing by his mother and brother.

Early in February 1961 Mr. Sternberg, a student in the University of Virginia, injured his back while lifting a motor scooter. On February 12th pain in his back became severe and extended into his left hip and leg and on the 13th he entered the University of Virginia Hospital for treatment. Examinations showed a ruptured intervertebral disc. This was removed surgically, and he was discharged from the hospital on March 22nd. A note on the hospital chart stated that at the time of admission the patient "appeared to be in moderate discomfort while walking with a left leg limp. The patient appeared extremely anxious during the examination and interview." I obtained the above facts and notes from the hospital records.

Mr. Sternberg's family lived in Brooklyn, New York, and as he did not want to disturb them unnecessarily he did not tell them either about his injury or his admission to the hospital. He even instructed his roommate, Mr. Arthur Weisman, to tell any callers that he was unavailable and studying in the library. Nevertheless, his mother, Mrs. Sarah Sternberg, became aware of her son's distress and admission to the hospital. The following note to me (undated, but received in March 1962), gives her own account of her impression:

> I had acquired and indulged in the luxury of reading in bed before retiring. It seems on this particular night I found

it difficult concentrating on the news, my thoughts kept drifting to Richard. I experienced a very anxious feeling, sort of an anxiety of his not being well. This caused me to become very restless and I felt a strong impulse to get out of bed and phone him. I controlled my emotions and the following day tried several times to reach him by phone. Either there was no answer or his roommate would not accept the calls, saying he was either in the library or in the hospital studying. This aroused my fears. After two days of continuously calling, I called the hospital and they confirmed my intuition. I immediately made plans to fly down to the hospital, as they could not connect me with my son. I called another friend of Richard's telling him that I was aware that he was in the hospital and not to withhold any information, but that I did not know the reason or cause of his confinement. He then told me that Richard was hurt while lifting a motor scooter, injury to his back, and he apologized for not answering the phone calls because Richard had told him not to alarm or worry his family.

Enclosed with Mrs. Sternberg's statement was a note from Richard himself, after he had consulted with her about the exact date on which she had first felt anxious:

Enclosed in this envelope you will find the letter which you have requested concerning what we had discussed in your office. However, I think this story is incomplete, for after this letter was sent by mother she recalled something she did not put down, hence called me and told me to make a note of it. The day before she called the hospital was February 14th, and she did not receive a Valentine's card from me, and this heightened her already [existing] suspicions. However, it is also interesting to note that throughout my seven years in Charlottesville, perhaps I sent her only one card. I did not send her a Valentine's card this year [1962] or my first year at the University either.

A further statement from Richard's brother, Roger, is dated November 19, 1962.

My mother had the initial premonition as to my brother Richard's injury. It was upon her insistence that I continued calling Richard and finally extracted the true story from his roommate.

With knowledge of his injury, my mother made the trip to Charlottesville and her initial intuition of hospitalization for my brother was correct.

Subsequently I sent Mrs. Sternberg a list of eight questions which she answered at length and returned with a letter dated November 16, 1962. The main points of her answers were that she had no idea her son had been engaging in any dangerous activity; she did not know he had been skiing or playing with a motor scooter, and she believed that she had become aware of her son's injury on the day it took place. This last item seems incorrect, however, since he was injured early in February, but he is said to have suffered no more than discomfort until February 12th, when severe pain developed. His mother is reported as actually calling the hospital on February 15th. But by then she had been trying to reach her son for two days and her alarm had increased when she did not receive a Valentine's Day card from him on February 14th. This would place her initial major impression of his being in trouble on February 12th, which was the day the pain in his back became severe and the day before his admission to the hospital. However, in response to a further question, Mrs. Sternberg said she had not told her other son, Roger, until "several days later," that is, after the impression of something being wrong with Richard had developed.

It seems doubtful whether Mrs. Sternberg's failure to receive a Valentine's card on February 14th has much importance. She herself stated that her anxiety began before February 14th and Richard Sternberg also pointed out that his mother had no special reason to expect a card from him since he did not send one the year before she had the impression. Furthermore, in response to a later inquiry from me as to how often she expected to hear from her son, Mrs. Sternberg wrote (December 27, 1962): "This year since the semester started [i.e., about three months], he has written me three letters in addition to occasional long distance telephone calls." From this it would seem that she did not expect to hear either often or regularly and that she had no reason for concern at the time she first felt anxious.

In the same letter Mrs. Sternberg also replied to another question from me regarding imagery: "I had no visual aspects of exactly what had happened. I just felt something unfavorable had happened to Richard and that due to the occurrence he was in the hospital. I did not see him lying in the hospital bed."

The hospital records stated that Mr. Richard Sternberg had had one previous admission to a hospital (also the University of Virginia Hospital) a year earlier, but apparently Mrs. Sternberg had no unusual experience at that time. Although she has had other experiences of what she describes as "intuitions" with regard to members of her family, she wrote on October 24, 1963: ". . . this was the only important occasion that I experienced when I knew there was something seriously wrong with Richard."

In later correspondence with Mr. Sternberg I posed the following question: "Has your mother had an impression of something being wrong with you, such as an illness, an accident, or other calamity, when, in fact, you were getting along quite well?"

In a letter dated January 5, 1965 Dr. Sternberg (as he then had become) replied as follows:

> In response to your inquiry regarding my mother's "impressions," she seems to me to be generally over-concerned about my health and well-being. However, on certain occasions this concern, which she calls "a premonition," seems to become magnified and results in actions comparable to the one you heard about when I had my back injury in Virginia. On these occasions she is seldom incorrect.

It appears from this statement that Mrs. Sternberg did sometimes become inappropriately anxious about her son, but she was credited by her family with being right in her statements about his condition most of the time. Mrs. Sternberg herself regarded the experience here reported as being unique with regard to her knowledge that something "seriously wrong" had happened to her son. And Dr. Sternberg himself in another letter to me (undated, but received in August, 1969) stated: "Other than the incident you know about, I cannot recall any time my mother claimed I was in the hospital."

Although Dr. Sternberg wished to keep his family from knowing that he had been injured, he was in fact thinking of them. In the letter quoted above, he said: "While in the hospital I thought of my mother often. I wanted her to know I was hospitalized and I wanted to have her company. I knew, however, that she would be upset by my condition and, therefore, I did not tell her."

Case 4

I first learned about this case on August 10, 1963, in conversation with Mr. and Mrs. Charles Hughes, at their home in Stoke-on-Trent, Staffordshire, England. From notes made at the time, I wrote an account of it a few days later and sent this to the Hughes for their amendments and signatures. After a few changes of detail, the following account was returned, signed by Mrs. Rose May (Charles) Hughes on October 9, 1963:

> About four years ago, my husband and I were going to Crewe to visit a sister of my husband who lives at Crewe. As we got off the train at Crewe, I had a strong impression or urge that we should go on to Chester where my cousin lived. I felt my cousin needed me, but had no impression of why.
>
> I persuaded my husband that we should go on to Chester and [we] continued on the same train to Chester and had to book [tickets] again at Chester.
>
> When we reached Chester and my cousin's house, my other cousin's husband who lived there answered the knock on the door and he said: "Oh, it's you, Rose. I'm glad you've come. Cissy wants to see you and we couldn't remember or find your address." Then when we went upstairs she [Mrs. Hughes' cousin] greeted me by saying: "Oh, Rose, I have been praying for you to come. I've lost your address." My cousin had recently become rather seriously ill with thrombosis and swelling of one leg. She was in bed and had had medical attention. But she had not been ill long and so far as I knew, before seeing her this time, she had been in good health. I had no reason to think she was ill. My cousin was single. We were very fond of each other.

Mr. Charles Hughes signed the following statement (also dated October 9, 1963):

> This is to state that I was a witness of the above events as I accompanied my wife on the trip she describes. I remember her saying we should change our plans and go on to Chester instead of staying in Crewe, and I remember her cousin saying she had prayed for my wife to come and had lost her address. So far as we knew, before we saw her, my wife's cousin had not been ill at that time.

In the previous conversation (August 1963) Mrs. Hughes had emphasized to me that her impression of being needed by her cousin in Chester did not include any visual images. She has had other experiences suggestive of extrasensory perception, including one of apparent precognition with imagery which I have published elsewhere (66, pp. 217-219).

Case 5

Although the next case occurred in 1938, many years before my investigation, it seems well supported by corroborating testimony. The percipient was Mrs. Ellen Vlok, Mount Catoggio, Piquetberg, Cape of Good Hope, Republic of South Africa, and her own account of it is given in the following letter dated October 21, 1963:

> Piquetberg, where I live, is a charming town about 80 miles from Cape Town.
>
> My daughter Elsa taught at the Albert Road School at Woodstock, living at a Sea Point hotel [near Cape Town]. This meant rising very early in the mornings, for she had to travel quite a long distance to her school.
>
> Elsa's regular, bright home letter arrived as usual on a certain Tuesday morning giving us full details of all her happy doings during the past week, in Cape Town. However, the next morning, Wednesday, I suddenly became unusually uneasy over her, and no matter how I tried to fight the feeling down, the conviction that something was amiss with Elsa grew stronger and stronger.

My husband and son, both solicitors, had already departed for the office, and what was their surprise when I burst in there, quite breathless, saying that something had gone wrong with Elsa and pleading that one of them should immediately take me to her—over 80 miles away. They both ridiculed the idea as just being my fanciful imagination. But I remained adamant, and eventually my son laughingly consented to leave [the] office to drive me to Sea Point at once.

There being no tarred national road at the time, a full two hours journey lay ahead. The nearer we drew to Cape Town, the more did I urge my son to drive faster and faster, and when we reached the hotel at 11:00 A.M., I rushed up the stairs to the second floor where her bedroom was, my son following. On opening the door, we found her pathetically perched in a queer position on the edge of her bed, still in her night clothes, numb with cold and unable to move at all, having slipped a disc in her spine as she was getting out of bed. Her calls for help had been futile, the maids only coming towards noon to do the rooms. Elsa had been in that taut position for more than four hours. We could not move her at all, so my son immediately rushed for a doctor, who could bring relief.

The above account was also signed as "quite true" by Miss Irene Walters, Mr. Vlok's secretary, who was in his office when Mrs. Vlok implored him and their son to take her to her daughter.

The daughter, Mrs. Elsa Sylvia Ross, who is the presumptive agent in this case, described her own recollection of it in a letter dated January 3, 1964, from which the following is an extract:

It must have been about 7:00 A.M., as I was dressing for school when I suddenly realized I could not straighten up. In great pain I tried to reach my bed to sit on the edge, but it was excruciating and if I remember correctly, I tried to change my position and slipped off on to the floor, from where I was unable to rise. I hoped someone would call for me, but no such luck—also the hotel maid did not reach the room until after my mother had put in an appearance about 11:00 A.M. No, I cannot recall praying for help from my mother. As I was fairly comfortable I think I dozed off to sleep. I do, however, know that when my mother walked in, I was not one scrap surprised, nor emotionally upset. But I was extremely grateful when they, plus a doctor, got me comfortable again, and the School Principal was telephoned to explain my absence at school.

Readers may note a discrepancy between Mrs. Vlok's statement that her daughter was "on the edge of her bed" and Mrs. Ross' statement that she was on the floor. This was resolved when Mrs. Vlok, in reply to an inquiry from me, forwarded a statement by Mrs. Ross as follows: "The bed was low. I could not get up out of it, so thought if I rolled to the edge and got my feet off, I'd manage better, only to find I could not, and then slipped on to the floor, from which I could not rise due to the terrific cramp in neck, shoulders and further down."

At my request, Mrs. Vlok's son, Mr. P. V. Vlok, also gave his recollections of the episode in the following letter dated April 17, 1964.

The incident happened more than 25 years ago and all I can really remember about it is that without prior warning my mother . . . made a very strong appeal that my father, to whom I was then articled, should allow me to drive her to Cape Town, as she had suddenly become very worried about my eldest sister, Sylvia. My father agreed to this and Mom and I left Piquetberg around about noon for the 85 mile drive to Cape Town. My sister was then staying in a beachfront hotel at Sea Point and on arrival there my mother and I went up to her bedroom which was on the first or second floor of the hotel. We found my sister, as far as I can remember, on the floor quite unable to reach the door or to attract anyone's attention.

The foregoing statements accord as to the main events, but include a discrepancy about times. Mr. P. V. Vlok stated that he and his mother did not leave Piquetberg until about noon, but Mrs. Vlok and her daughter stated that she and her son had arrived in Cape Town around 11:00 A.M. This discrepancy led to further correspondence in 1969 between me and the three informants. Mr. Vlok remained firm in his belief that he and his mother had not left Piquetberg until "shortly before noon" and could not have reached Cape Town (after driving 85 miles) until 2:00 P.M. or perhaps later. Mrs. Vlok, on reconsidering the matter, wrote that she now agreed with her son's remembrance of the times, but Mrs. Ross, the agent, thought that her brother was in error. She felt sure that he and her mother had at any rate arrived to help her before noon since the maid usually came in to do the room around noon and had not come in by the time they arrived. It seems probable that the actual time of arrival of the rescuers in Cape Town was somewhere in between the limits suggested in the different accounts.

Mr. Vlok (the percipient's husband) having died since the incident, I asked Mr. P. V. Vlok and Miss Walters (the senior Mr. Vlok's former secretary) whether they had ever known Mrs. Vlok to plead to be taken to her daughter on any other occasion. Miss Walters replied on November 21, 1963: "I cannot remember [that] Mrs. Vlok ever persuaded her husband to make any unnecessary trips."

Mr. P. V. Vlok wrote on April 27, 1964, that "I cannot at all recall my mother at any stage having made similar statements. In fact, I can dispel immediately any suggestion that she is an imaginative person. She is highly intelligent, practical in her outlook and in her thoughts, and certainly not given to all sorts of suggestions."

On being asked whether she had experienced any imagery on this occasion, Mrs. Vlok replied on January 3, 1964, that "I just had a distinct conviction, with no specific details, that something had happened to Elsa—that she was in trouble—with a strong urge that I should go to her at once."

In the letter quoted above, Miss Walters had also commented that ". . . Mrs. Vlok expressed just a general impression that her daughter was in distress."

Mrs. Vlok has had only one other experience suggestive of extrasensory perception; this was also connected with a disaster to one of her children. A few years before the incident just described, she had a recurrent auditory, or at least verbal, thought: "What if John gets taken away?" This coincided with the sudden, quite unexpected and fatal illness of another son, John, who was miles away in Pietermaritzburg and, so far as Mrs. Vlok knew, in perfect health.

Case 6

The next case is one of four in this main group of cases which lacks corroboration of the telling of the experience before the related events became known to the percipient.

M. Miltiade Rhally (a clinical psychologist of Zurich) described the following impression in an unpublished account of paranormal experiences which was lent to me by a mutual friend. The episode occurred in 1962 while M. Rhally was away from his home in Zurich. The following account was written some months after the experience and related event:

> I had just finished my day of work and was walking in the park of the clinic where I practice when the thought flashed through my mind: "Something has happened to Yorgo (the eldest of my three children)—telephone to Zurich!" This impulse to inquire about my son I perceived so clearly that I looked at my watch to note the time. But when, a few minutes later, I arrived near a telephone the sense of urgency had subsided and I therefore dropped the matter. Nevertheless, on arriving home the next day at noon, my first words were to ask my wife [whether] anything had happened yesterday to Yorgo. Whereupon I was told that they had been to look at a traditional Zurich event (*Verbrennung des Boogs*) and that Yorgo had lost himself in the crowd. At the time I thought of him he had been taken to the police station, where my wife went to fetch him a while later!

Shortly after reading M. Rhally's account, I met him in Zurich. We talked about it briefly and I asked if Mme Rhally could corroborate it. I have translated the following extracts from her letter in French, dated February 22, 1964:

> With regard to the episode mentioned by my husband, here is what I remember:
> In April or May, 1962, I was present with my two children

at the traditional parade of *Sechseläute,* at the end of which the figure of man symbolizing winter is set on fire on a stake.

My son Yorgo, complaining that he could not see well enough, with my permission slid through the crowd to the front row of spectators while I held the younger child on my shoulders.

When the celebration had ended, the crowd dispersed, but Yorgo had disappeared in the confusion, not knowing where to find me again, although I had remained where I was. It was then about 6:30 P.M.

After waiting twenty minutes very nervously, I went to a policeman who persuaded us to go to the police bureau where, in fact, Yorgo was waiting with three or four other strayed children.

We went home. I then got a telephone call from a colleague of my husband who works at the same place and I told him about the events of the afternoon.

I do not think on that evening that I received a telephone call from my husband or tried to call him myself, because he had to attend a conference lasting well into the night and was not expected back from the clinic until noon of the following day.

. . . I am quite certain that when he came home the next day, my husband told me he had had the very distinct impression the previous evening between 6:30 and 7:00 P.M. that something had happened to Yorgo.

However, he had not telephoned at that time, which would not in any case have accomplished anything, since I was at that moment trying to find my son.

The clinic where M. Rhally works and where he was at the time of his impression, is some fifty kilometers from Zurich where Yorgo and his mother then were.

In reply to further inquiries, M. Rhally said he was quite sure that his impression came while he was walking in a park with a friend between 6:00 P.M., when he finished work, and 7:00 P.M., when he had his evening meal. (It will be noted that although with a friend, he may well have been more or less passive, relaxing after work.) He could not identify the time more precisely, although he had looked at his watch in order to do so.

As it seemed possible that M. Rhally's colleague, who had

heard the story of Yorgo's misadventure from Mme Rhally, might have told M. Rhally about it when they met the next day, M. and Mme Rhally consulted this colleague and their own memories again. The colleague then asserted, and M. Rhally remembered, that they had met at work that morning and that he had mentioned hearing about the incident from Mme Rhally. M. Rhally did not tell his colleague about his own impression, and the first other person to hear about it was his wife on his return home about noon the same day. The evidential weakness of this case, then, is that the percipient did not speak of his impression until *after* he had heard of the related event by normal means.

M. and Mme Rhally both stated that on no other occasion when returning home had M. Rhally asked if anything unusual had happened to Yorgo—beyond, that is, his natural inquiries for family news.

M. Rhally had had only one other impression experience at all resembling the one just described, and this was possibly symbolic. While his children were staying with their grandparents in Freiburg, he dreamed that the burner of a stove was glowing red; this caused him, first thing the next morning, to telephone and inquire after the children. He was told that the second child, Nicholas, had developed a high fever the night before.

Case 7

In the next case the percipient was Dr. Asad Masri, a psychiatric resident at the University of Virginia (at the time of the experience) and a person well known to me. His wife, Mrs. Linda Masri, was with her husband on the occasion and I talked with them both about it in Charlottesville. Each furnished written statements. I give first that written by Mrs. Masri. Her account which follows is dated November 21, 1964:

> About the second week of June [1964] my husband and I decided to go and visit the Paul Travis' to see their new daughter and deliver a gift.
>
> My mother's mother was visiting us at the time and had kept the babies several times so this was the plan for that night. Susie [Mrs. Masri's maternal grandmother] is seventy-six but

quite active and we felt quite responsible. We asked our neighbor across the hall to listen in case there was any difficulty since Susie did not know the area and [might] need to ask her something.

We drove over and Paul [Travis] met us at the door. We sat down after viewing the new baby and Paul began to show us his collection of Civil War money. He then began to show Asad the blueprints of his new home and I began to talk with Louise [Mrs. Travis]. We had drinks brought in by Paul and Asad suddenly said: "Linda, call home. I'm afraid something is wrong." I tended to ignore this and he became more persistent, at which point I said I'd call later since we had only been there about twenty minutes.

I did get up and go into the bedroom to call, still feeling no concern. Asad followed me, however, and I remember thinking this odd. When I called, my neighbor answered the phone saying that we had better get home since Susie had hurt her back and was very upset.

We went home immediately and found the children practically hysterical and Susie sitting with them but in great pain. Scott [the Masri's one-year-old son], was especially upset and refused to let me hold him but grabbed for Asad and calmed down soon after.

Asad said later that the feeling he had was that of anxiety; strangely enough, he felt that Scott was calling for him.

In questioning Susie as to what happened, I couldn't obtain much except that she had attempted to lift Scott out of the playpen and experienced severe back pain. Nadia (our daughter) was asleep and only began to cry later on. Apparently she [Susie] jolted or dropped Scott so that he was terribly frightened.

Dr. Asad Masri furnished the following separate account of his remembrance of the episode, dated November 15, 1964:

Around the middle of June, 1964, Linda and I decided to visit the Travis' to congratulate them on their new child. After supper we put the children to bed and we asked Linda's grandmother to babysit for a while.

We arrived there and Paul Travis fixed our drinks. As he

was showing me the blueprints of his new house I stopped and had a feeling as if something bad had happened at home, the nature of which I was not aware.

I asked Linda to call home. She said: "I will in a few minutes." I said: "You'd better call now. Something is wrong."

Linda went to the bedroom where the phone was and I followed and my feelings then were of distress. Our . . . neighbor answered the phone. Both children were screaming in the background. She informed us that Linda's grandmother had hurt her back just [a] few minutes earlier and [that] the children were so frightened. . . .

We arrived home and the neighbor met us at the door, saying that Linda's grandmother had called upon [her] after she hurt her back.

Scott, my son, was frantic and refused to go to Linda and clutched me for comfort.

What is surprising about this incident is the sudden feeling of distress and my insistence on Linda to call home and my premonition that something [had] happened at home.

In response to questions about details of this experience, Dr. and Mrs. Masri furnished further relevant information: Both agreed that Dr. Masri had on some earlier occasions shown evidence of apparent extrasensory perception. The most important incident they remembered had to do with a prediction of their receiving urgently needed money which they had no rational grounds for expecting would come. Both agreed that Dr. Masri had never had a strong impression (such as the present one) that something was wrong at home (or elsewhere) when in fact nothing was wrong. Mrs. Masri stated that Dr. Masri had never before asked her to telephone home when they were away. It was their custom to telephone home and talk to the babysitter, but only after they had been away for two or three hours. On this occasion they had barely arrived at their hosts' house when Dr. Masri began pressing his wife to telephone home.

Mrs. Masri's grandmother had given no previous indication of having pain in her back. Hence there were no rational grounds for the Masris to expect this, or that she would drop or jolt the child.

From the information Mrs. Masri obtained from her neighbor, she judged that Dr. Masri's impression had coincided (to within a few minutes) with the time when Mrs. Masri's grandmother developed pain and the little boy became frightened after she (apparently) dropped him.

Readers will note that Mrs. Masri stated that her husband said he "felt that Scott was calling for him." Dr. Masri himself (five months after the episode) could not remember this more specific detail. He could only remember that he was sure something was wrong at home. Both Dr. and Mrs. Masri agree, however, that when they reached home the little boy showed a preference to go to Dr. Masri rather than to Mrs. Masri. Mrs. Masri did not think that her husband showed any preference for one of their children in particular.

In this case there were two possible agents since both the frightened child and Mrs. Masri's grandmother could have acted in this role.

Case 8

In the next case the percipient was Mr. Edward R. Harrow of Hardyville, Virginia. His wife, Mrs. Beverly Harrow, has herself had a number of apparent extrasensory experiences which she described to me in an interview in Charlottesville and in subsequent correspondence. In the course of this correspondence, she wrote me on September 29, 1965, about an experience of her husband, as follows:

> The . . . incident occurred July 17th [1965] at my sister's wedding reception. I was serving punch; my husband was dutifully taking care of window fans, etc. He was talking with my brother (the two . . . are very congenial), when (he told me later) . . . he felt something was wrong at home. We had left our children with his mother and . . . with his sister. He immediately left [the] reception and went to my father's home and called his mother. His mother said on the phone that our nineteen month old baby was ill with a very high fever and she had been watching the clock for an hour, thinking about what we were doing and at what time she could get in touch with us. She didn't want

to disturb us, but was very concerned as the doctor was out of town. We left the reception immediately and drove home to find the baby indeed very ill with a throat and ear infection and a fever of 106°.

I talked with my mother-in-law after things settled down and she said that at 5:30 P.M. she was concentrating on calling me and the phone rang and it was Edward. We were all glad that Edward called when he did because otherwise we would have been an hour or so later getting home.

To the best of my knowledge the baby was in good health when we left him with my mother-in-law. We had been gone from the baby about twenty-four hours before my husband called his mother.

Mr. Edward R. Harrow signed the following statement: "To the best of my knowledge the above accords with my recollection of this episode."

This is another case in which two persons (here the baby and the grandmother) could have acted as agents. One of these presumptive agents, the grandmother, was, so to speak, aiming her message at her daughter-in-law, Mrs. Beverly Harrow, but it was her son who got the impression that something was wrong. Yet Mrs. Harrow herself has had a number of apparently paranormal experiences on other occasions.

Case 9

Although the next case is an old one, it is of a type where errors of memory are perhaps improbable and it is corroborated by the testimony of the percipient's daughter, Mrs. Benedict J. McGillis, who reported it verbally to me at Mt. Edgecumbe, Alaska, in July, 1965. I made notes about the case immediately after our interview. From these I wrote an account and sent it to Mrs. McGillis, requesting her to ask her mother, Mrs. Eleanor A. Jensen, to sign it after making any amendments they felt necessary.

Mrs. McGillis did not visit her mother, who lives in Nebraska, for some months, but eventually they both signed the statement, unamended, on July 26, 1966, and returned it to me with a letter dated August 8, 1966. The signed statement giving the account of Mrs. McGillis, follows:

When I was about seven or eight years old, my maternal grandparents died. This occurred about 1930. My family was then living in Belden, Nebraska. I was born in 1923.

One day I noticed that my mother was weeping while she was doing the housework, and particularly the ironing. Tears from her face fell onto the clothes she was ironing. I asked her why she was crying and she said, "Because Grandma and Grandpa are dead." I then said, "No, they are both fine. They are in Coleridge [Nebraska]." Mother said in reply, "No, not Grandma and Grandpa Jensen, but Grandma and Grandpa Larsen." [The Larsen grandparents were in Denmark.] As I recall, my mother began crying in the morning.

Later on, I learned that Mother had continued weeping all day. In the evening, my father came upstairs from the downstairs grocery store which he kept and handed a cable to my mother. He had received the cable about 3 P.M. and had delayed going upstairs to give it to Mother. He did not want to give her the bad news until he had to do so, when he had to go upstairs at the end of the working day. When my father did give the cable to my mother, she said, "You don't have to tell me what is in it. Mama and papa are dead."

The cable did, in fact, say that Grandma Larsen had died in her sleep and Grandpa died a few hours later of a broken heart.

My mother never told me how she received the impression of her parents' deaths. She did not say it came in a dream. My grandparents had died the day before I saw my mother weeping, and it took about a day for the news to reach us in Nebraska. My grandparents were living in Denmark when they died.

My mother had never at any other time said that her parents had died and, in fact, they had never been ill at all until the day they died. My maternal grandfather was ninety-nine and my maternal grandmother ninety-six at the time they died. They were both thought to be in good health and, although elderly, there was absolutely no reason to believe that they were going to die in the near future at the time my mother had her impression that they had died.

Since Mrs. McGillis was a small girl at the time of this incident many years before, I requested also a statement from Mr. Jensen, the percipient's husband. Unfortunately, at the time of my inquiries in 1965 to 1967 Mr. Jensen was an elderly gentleman. Although his daughter reported to me in a letter dated August 8, 1966, that he "had agreed with my mother that my recollections were totally correct," he was reluctant to sign the statement at that time. Mrs. McGillis wrote me later that her father was unusually cautious about all legal appearing documents! I persisted in requesting some statement from Mr. Jensen and eventually he signed one which was sent to me by Mrs. McGillis with a letter dated March 13, 1967. The statement was as follows:

> I, Jens Andrew Jensen, do hereby certify that the incidents recalled and related by my wife—Eleanora Augusta Larsen Jensen—are true facts and that they actually did happen, in her impressions of the death of her parents—who resided in Denmark at the time they died on the same day; and in her impressions of her sister's death. Neither of these impressions were received during sleep or dream states. My wife told me she actually felt and saw these things, more like a vision than a dream. She knew in both cases most of the particulars, and the certainty of death, before I could bring the cabled messages to her.

Mrs. McGillis had previously written me (in her letter of August 8, 1966) about her mother's other apparently paranormal experience mentioned in Mr. Jensen's statement. She wrote that one night Mrs. Jensen felt that her sister, Marie, then living in Norway while she herself was in the United States, "had wakened her and stood beside her bed as she waved good-bye to Mother [Mrs. Jensen] from what appeared to be the deck of a steamer." This experience coincided with Marie's death.

Mr. Jensen's statement suggests that his wife had visual images in both her experiences. The second experience related to the death of Mrs. Jensen's sister Marie does seem to have taken the form of a waking visual apparition. But the first experience, according to my notes of my interview with Mrs. McGillis and the statement signed by Mrs. Jensen and Mrs. McGillis, seems to have been an impression without visual imagery.

Case 10

For the following case I am indebted to Mrs. Rosalind Heywood, to whom it was sent by the percipient who had heard a broadcast talk on extrasensory perception by Mrs. Heywood. Subsequently I corresponded with the percipient and obtained a partial corroboration from her husband. Strictly speaking, this case is not corroborated with regard to the percipient having had her experience before she gained normal knowledge of the related events. But, as will be seen, her extraordinary action taken on the strength of the impression, which is corroborated by her husband, provides a confirmation that she did have such an impression.

The percipient, Mrs. Mary O'Brien (pseudonym) of Manchester, England, wrote as follows in a letter of June 30, 1960:

> My husband is manager of a large ice cream factory which . . . was located about two and a half miles away. . . . I was accustomed to him coming home any time between 11 P.M. and 6 A.M., so I was never worried if he was late.
>
> One Saturday evening last December [1959], expecting him to be late, I settled down to watch the TV, but couldn't settle. After a while I phoned the depot but got no reply and assumed my husband was out, but still could not settle. After phoning unsuccessfully three times, I decided at 2 A.M. to walk to the depot. This I did; there was no reply and the door was locked, but feeling even more uneasy for no apparent reason, I took it upon myself to break a window and climb in. I found my husband locked in the cold store [walk-in refrigerator] and, on comparing notes, discovered that it had happened only minutes before I felt I had to phone the first time. Needless to say, had I not had this premonition my husband might well have suffered seriously from the effects of a night in the cold store.

Mr. Dennis O'Brien countersigned this account as correct. In reply to questions from Mrs. Heywood, Mrs. O'Brien wrote later, on October 6, 1960:

> My feeling that I could not settle can only be explained as "butterflies in my tummy," making it almost impossible for me

to sit and concentrate on anything, rather as one feels before a dentist's appointment.

I had never worried about my husband before, even when his work kept him out till 6 in the morning. (I simply went to bed and slept.) Nor have I ever worried since. I might add that the night I went to the depot I took the risk of leaving my two-months-old daughter in her bed alone, something I would never have done under normal conditions and something I have never done since.

Mr. O'Brien commented on this statement: "It is quite true that my wife had never before shown any signs of distress or worry however late I returned home—often as late as 6 A.M."

In subsequent correspondence with Mrs. O'Brien I learned of another experience she had had. In this instance she again became uneasy when her husband was away from home but not expected back soon and thus not overdue in returning. Her uneasiness increased over several days until eventually she telephoned his head office and learned that he had had an accident and been hospitalized. Since I do not have corroboration of this experience, I shall not include its details here. I mention it, however, because it permits inclusion of Mrs. O'Brien in the fairly large group of percipients who have had more than one apparently paranormal experience during their lifetimes.

Case 11

The next case was reported to me by the percipient, Mrs. Joicey Acker Hurth, who sent me the following account of her experience enclosed in a letter dated May 24, 1967:

I was still a happy bride of three months until that night in 1949 when my feeling of ecstasy suddenly turned into a mood of depression. There was no logical reason for it at the time. This day, as others preceding it, was filled with enthusiasm in relation to my adjustment to the community life of Cedarburg, Wisconsin, a delightful small city just north of Milwaukee.

My husband and I were temporarily living with his parents, Dr. and Mrs. O. J. Hurth. Although I was separated from my former home, Anderson, South Carolina, by a thousand miles in distance, I did not feel lonely or homesick because my sister was married to my husband's brother and lived nearby. We were very close. Also, I felt much at home with my in-laws and was treated as a member of the family.

It must have been sometime after midnight, January 23 [1949] when I awakened with a feeling of deep sadness, an impression that something was wrong. I did not want to disturb my husband, so for a long while I stared wide-eyed at the ceiling of the bedroom which was barely visible in a dim, shadowy light. I remember the terrible ache in my heart. I started to cry and sobbed softly into my pillow. My husband was immediately awake and asked many questions to which I had no answers. I repeated over and over to him that I had a feeling that something was wrong. His efforts to console me were futile and I did not sleep the rest of the night.

The next morning when we went downstairs to breakfast my in-laws were shocked at my appearance—swollen red eyes and haggard expression. They accused us of having had a "lovers' quarrel," but I assured them that this was not the case. I told them I had no explanation for my mood of depression. They were much concerned.

I put bread into the toaster and while waiting for it I suddenly wheeled around and exclaimed, "It's my father! Something is terribly wrong with my father!"

I had no reason for my statement. My father was a man of robust health for his sixty-nine years and had known little illness in his entire life.

Each one speaking in turn tried to tell me that it was my imagination. My mother-in-law reminded me of the letter I had received from my father only a few days before and he had made no mention of an illness.

"No," I said. "I'm sure. I must go home!"

The telephone rang while I was speaking, and although this was a doctor's home where the telephone rang constantly, I knew this call was for me and answered it.

My aunt spoke first, telling me that my father was in a coma and was dying. Then my mother took the phone and asked, "Didn't you receive my letter? I wrote you that your father was very ill."

I told her I had received no letter from her. (I later learned that all planes had been grounded because of bad weather and the mail was held up.)

The conversation that followed was an explanation of my father's sudden illness. He had taken a sulfa drug for a backache. His regular physician was not in the office, and the drug was given to him by a male nurse and without the caution to drink plenty of water.

Before he had finished the tablets given him his skin began to turn a purplish color and he became very ill. He was taken to Anderson County Hospital and tests showed that the drug had caused crystallization in the kidneys. They could not function properly. In spite of all efforts made to save him, he lived about a week before his body was consumed with poison. The last few days he was in a deep coma.

Because of a heavy snowstorm no planes were taking off, so my sister and I took a train. I had been warned that it was possible that my father would not live until I got there. I had the feeling that he would. On arrival we took a taxi directly to the hospital where all the family had gathered. I was told by a doctor that it was not likely that my father would ever come out of the coma. Again, I had the strong feeling that he would and would know that I was there. While others in the family waited in a private room I sat beside his bed and held his hand. He was in an oxygen tent and his hands were cold. I sat there for about a half hour. Finally, he stirred. I ran to get the other members of the family. With all of us around his bed he opened his eyes. There was recognition in them though he could not speak. He raised his head completely off the pillow, waved his arms in a circular motion, smiled (it seemed that he smiled when he saw me); then his head fell back as he gasped his last breath.

I still do not know whether my impression of my father's illness was telepathy between him—in his unconscious state— and me, or between my worried mother and me. At any rate, I deeply felt the urgency of the situation in spite of the distance of separation, not from any visual image but strictly as an emotional reaction to some crisis.

Mr. R. P. Hurth furnished the following corroboration of his wife's experience in a letter to me dated April 21, 1968:

> I well remember the morning of which my wife speaks concerning the awareness of her father's illness. On awakening from a sound sleep, I became aware of my wife sobbing. While trying to console her, I asked her why she was crying. Her answer was, "I don't know." Later at the breakfast table my father, who was a physician and surgeon, questioned my wife to ascertain whether or not there were any physical pains which might have caused her crying. After a few moments she cried out that something was very wrong with her father. Thereupon my father tried to reassure her that nothing was wrong. He said, "If there were anything wrong with your father, we would have heard something from Anderson either by letter or phone." He had no sooner finished saying [this] when the telephone rang. The caller was my wife's aunt calling from Anderson, S.C. She told her that her father was very ill.

I then put three additional questions to Mr. Hurth, which he answered as follows on May 26, 1967:

Q. Was this the occasion when your wife's father had his final illness? What was the date (approximately or exact) of this experience and your father-in-law's illness?

A. Yes, my father-in-law, William David Acker, Sr., died at the Anderson County Hospital, Anderson, S.C., on January 25, 1949. My wife had this experience some few days prior to his death.

Q. Had your wife on any other occasions claimed that her father was ill?

A. No; to my knowledge her father had not been ill at all since our marriage in October 1948 at which time I was in the home in Anderson, S.C. and had personal contact with him. He seemed perfectly well at that time.

Q. Did you or your wife have any reason to believe that your father-in-law was ill or was likely to become ill at the time of her experience?

A. No, none whatsoever.

In response to a further question from me, Mr. Hurth wrote

me again in a letter dated October 12, 1968, as follows: "Up until the day of the phone call from Anderson, S. C., informing Joicey [Mrs. Hurth] about her father being in the hospital, I had always thought of Mr. Acker as being a healthy, robust individual. I had never heard anything to the contrary."

The last sentence in Mr. Hurth's letter quoted above was in response to my question as to whether Mrs. Hurth had had other (incorrect) impressions or forebodings that her father was ill or dying. His response did not, however, answer the question whether Mrs. Hurth had sometimes claimed that her father was ill when he was not. Mr. Hurth dealt with this point in another statement, dated October 24, 1968: "To the best of my knowledge my wife never told me that her father was in poor health, ill, or dying from the time I first knew her up until the occasion on January 23, 1949, when my wife told us one day at breakfast that there was something 'terribly wrong' with her father."

Mrs. Hurth also sent me a photostat copy of a letter she had received from her mother-in-law, Mrs. Oscar J. Hurth, with whom she had been staying at the time she had the impression of her father's illness. The letter, dated October 28, 1964, includes the following statements:

> I recalled the morning that you came down to breakfast, red-eyed and upset. You told us about the feeling you had about [your father] being very sick. Dad and I tried to convince you that you had had a nightmare. We also mentioned that your letter from your father, a few days previous, hadn't mentioned any illness. While we were talking the telephone rang. It was a call from your mother saying that your father was desperately ill.
>
> Dad asked you for the name of your family doctor and called him at the hospital. The doctor said that your father's kidneys weren't functioning due to a sulfa drug to which he was allergic.

Mrs. Hurth has had several other experiences suggestive of extrasensory perception. Subsequent to the correspondence quoted above, I visited her and her family in Cedarburg, Wisconsin, and talked with them about Mrs. Hurth's paranormal experiences. She had had six definite impression experiences, of which five were corroborated and verified by members of her family. Her father was agent in one (Case 11), her daughter agent in three (Cases 12, 29, and 32), and her son agent in two. In the cases in which her daughter was agent she was involved in some kind of accident, but when her son was agent he was on both occasions engaged in an activity his mother disapproved of and which he had concealed from her. Mrs. Hurth has also had a single striking, but non-veridical, apparitional experience of her deceased brother. In spite of her numerous paranormal experiences, when a beloved sister was tragically killed in a fire in another town, Mrs. Hurth had no paranormal awareness of her death. And although, as already stated, she had paranormal experiences on three occasions when her daughter was injured or in an accident, on a fourth occasion of injury to her daughter, she had no such experience.

I have included three other cases in which Mrs. Hurth is the percipient in this monograph and the next case is the first of these.

Case 12

In this case, which occurred in 1955, Mrs. Hurth became aware of an accident in which her little daughter, Joicey, was involved. Mrs. Hurth sent me an account in a letter dated October 11, 1968, as follows:

> When my five-year-old daughter came home from a birthday party, she was disappointed to find that her father and brother had gone to the Walt Disney movie without her. The Rivoli Theater is a block and a half away on the main street (Washington Ave.) which runs parallel with Portland Ave., our home address. I told Joicey that her father expected her to join them there, so she waved goodbye and skipped towards the corner.
>
> I returned to the dinner dishes still unwashed in the kitchen sink. Quite suddenly while I held a plate in my hand an awesome feeling came over me. I dropped the plate, turned my eyes towards heaven and prayed aloud, "Oh, God, don't let her get killed!"
>
> For some unexplainable reason I knew Joicey had been hit by a car or was going to be. I was quite conscious of her

involvement in an accident. I immediately went to the telephone, looked up a number, and shakily dialed the theater. I gave my name and said, "My little girl was on the way to the theater. She has had an accident. Is she badly hurt?"

The girl answering the telephone stammered, "How did you know? It—the accident—just happened. Hold the phone please!"

While I held the receiver, waiting, the siren sounded and an ambulance went out. I was frantic. Soon a very calm voice, that of the manager, Ray Nichols, spoke, "Mrs. Hurth, your little girl was struck by a car, but she is all right. Your husband is with her now. She appears to be in good shape, only stunned. Your husband is taking her to Dr. Hurth [little Joicey's uncle] now for an examination. Incidentally, Mrs. Hurth, how did you know?"

I don't remember my reply to this question; probably I said that I had a strong feeling that something had happened.

Another call to Dr. Hurth's home assured me that Joicey had not been seriously hurt. She had run into a moving car, was bounced off the front left fender to the pavement, had gotten up herself and run back to the same side of the street from which she started and sat on the curb until someone came. Dr. Hurth suggested that my husband take her to the movie anyway to get her mind off the accident. I did not see her until some two hours later. She had a few facial bruises, a swollen lip and a dirty party dress, but was otherwise fine.

Joicey remembers that at the time she was hit she called, "Mama." She remembers sitting on the curb crying and calling "Mama, Mama, I want my Mama."

Although Mrs. Hurth did not send me the above full account of this incident until October, 1968, in previous letters she and her daughter and husband had alluded to it. Mrs. Hurth's daughter, Joicey, the agent of this episode, wrote her recollection of the episode to me in a letter dated April 19, 1968, as follows:

Relating to the incident of my slight accident with a car, I believe I can add something . . . After I was struck, I was very stunned, but I managed to run blindly through a back alley in

the direction of home. I can distinctly remember screaming inaudibly [sic] "Mama! Mama!" I don't believe I made any sound
because I was so terrified, but before the driver of the car stopped
me, I made a silent plea for my mother that I believe she
received.

Mr. R. P. Hurth, the percipient's husband, remembered the
episode also and in a letter to me of April 21, 1967, mentioned his
memories of it as follows:

Another instance . . . I well remember because if I had
waited for my daughter before going to the theater, my daughter
might not have run into the car. I was sitting beside my son in
the theater when the manager of the theater asked me to step
into the lobby. On entering the lobby I was informed that my
daughter had just run into a car in front of the building and
that she was sitting between two buildings across the street.

In Case 29 (see Chapter IV) Mrs. Hurth did not connect
an impression of pain she had with either of her children specifically,
although she did ask them when they came home from school if
anything unusual had happened to them. In the present case, however, Mrs. Hurth definitely associated her impression with Joicey
as she indicates in the following statement dated September 18,
1968, but sent with her letter of October 11, 1968:

When Joicey was struck by a car it was a little different in
this respect. I connected the impression I had of an accident
directly with Joicey. I did not see or have a mental image of a
car hitting Joicey, but I did have the impression so strongly
that I did not question it or hesitate to call the theater to inquire. Although I did know she had been hit, I did not know
to what extent, if any, she had been injured.

On the occasion of my visit to Cedarburg in 1969 I examined
the terrain of this case, walking between the Hurth house and the
Rivoli Theater outside which Joicey L. Hurth had been hit by a
passing car. I also talked with the theater manager, Mr. Ray
Nichols, who remembered the incident quite well.

Mr. Nichols corroborated that Mrs. Hurth had telephoned the theater and asked about an accident involving her daughter only one or two minutes after it happened. He did not remember whether he had himself spoken with Mrs. Hurth, but thought this possible. The telephone was in the cashier's booth and was answered first by her. He was sure there was no time for anyone to have run and told Mrs. Hurth about the accident after it happened and before she telephoned.

I considered the possibility that Mrs. Hurth (a block and half away from the theater) might have heard the sound of screeching brakes and, knowing that her daughter was on the street, might have associated the noise with danger to her daughter. In talking about this possibility, Mrs. Hurth denied that she had heard any screeching of brakes and Mr. Nichols thought it impossible for such a sound, if it had occurred, to have been heard at Mrs. Hurth's house. The street is rather narrow and cars always proceed slowly along it. The sort of tire screech that sometimes occurs in highway accidents at high speeds was not possible in this case. Nor could Mrs. Hurth have heard Joicey because the little girl was stunned and her call to her mother ("screaming inaudibly," as she called it) was mental rather than vocal.

Mr. Hurth, incidentally, was a second corroborator of his wife's impression, since he said that he heard at the theater (but did not remember from whom) that his wife had telephoned about the accident immediately after it happened.

Case 13

The following case was first reported to me by Mrs. Brigitte Judd, of Upland, California, who is also the percipient in a case reported later in this monograph (Case 34). In the present case her husband, Mr. J. W. Judd, is the percipient. I will present first Mrs. Judd's account of the experience which she sent me in a letter dated January 9, 1968, as follows:

On Tuesday, December 18, 1967, a friend of mine who lives in an apartment just across the yard from me . . . invited me to have a cup of coffee with her. This was at about 10 A.M.

My two older children, a girl nine and a boy eight, were home on vacation. My youngest child, Dumpling, a girl, is four. I put the nine-year-old in charge for a few minutes and went to have my cup of coffee. At about 10:15 A.M. my boy came running and told me that Puppy (our Dachshund female) bit Dumpling. I ran into my apartment with him. The four-year-old girl was screaming hysterically; the dog looked cowed and crouched in her corner.

Naturally I was upset. My four-year-old usually walked with that dog. She played with the dog all the time. Now the dog had bitten her! I first calmed the little girl down and determined that the "bite" was mostly a large bruise on her mouth that slowly turned dark blue. There were only her own teeth-marks on the inside of her lip. The two older children confirmed that the dog had growled and snapped at her though.

All this time I thought strongly of my husband and what he would say and do. Fifteen minutes later—at 10:30 A.M. as my wristwatch showed—the telephone rang. My husband called and said: "What's wrong? I know something has happened. Tell me, what's going on?"

I was still a little dazed or maybe in some sort of shock, because I replied airily: "Oh, nothing. Puppy just bit the Dumpling, that's all." He then told me that he had been on his way back to his office from a business trip about 100 miles from our home. His office is about 20 miles from our home, but there is a toll charge on telephone calls and we do not usually call one another. So, he was somewhere between 100 and 120 miles from me when the bite occurred and he drove back to the office at top speed, calling home just as soon as he reached his telephone. He told me that he nearly jumped out of his skin because he just knew that something awful had happened.

At my request Mr. Judd, the percipient, sent me his own account of this experience in a letter dated February 3, 1968, as follows:

As to what happened on Tuesday, December 18, 1967, I had to go to San Diego on business. It was raining extremely hard when I left the Los Angeles area, and this caused me to reach San Diego much later than I had anticipated. I was late

for my appointment and felt quite uneasy because of it; however, the sun was bright and the weather clear when I finally
reached San Diego and I had no further reason to worry, since
my business was concluded successfully. The uneasy feeling
deepened on my return trip. As I drove north the weather
cleared ahead of me, but my apprehension did not. I just became
more and more worried over nothing in particular. When I
reached the office, I could contain myself no longer and I
called home. The only thing I could think to say to my wife was,
"What's going on?"

In reply to further questions which I sent, Mrs. Judd wrote
in a letter dated March 3, 1968, as follows:

In reply to your letter of February 12, 1968, I can tell you
that my husband has not called me more than five or six
times during the last year. He usually has some brief message to
give me or asks if some matter pertaining to his business has
arrived there. The call in question was the first time that he
merely said: "What's going on?"

In response to a further question from me Mrs. Judd wrote
on June 24, 1969 as follows: "There has been no other time that
Celeste [Dumpling] or any other member of this family suffered a
fright similar to the dog incident when my husband has not called
home."

I was able to interview Mr. and Mrs. Judd in their home in
Upland, California. We reviewed some of the details of this experience, including the distance Mr. Judd had traveled on the
morning it occurred.

Mr. Judd stated that he sometimes would leave to drive to
San Diego as early as 6.30 A.M. He could then easily drive there
from Upland, finish some business, and return to his office (which
is about fifteen or twenty miles west of Upland, closer to San
Diego) by 10.30 A.M. He could not recall clearly what his business in San Diego was on the day in question, but thought that a
man he had wanted to see was not available and so he had returned immediately after reaching that city. It is nevertheless impos-

sible that, as Mrs. Judd said in her written statement, Mr. Judd could have been a hundred miles from their home at the time the dog attacked their little girl (10:15 A.M.) and fifteen minutes later (10.30 A.M.) have telephoned from his office located about eighty miles from San Diego. Either he was closer to his office than Mrs. Judd thought or she was wrong about the time of his telephone call. This point is not, however, critical for evaluating the case as an instance of extrasensory perception.

Another matter, however, is critical and this is the frequency with which Mr. Judd telephoned his home to ask what was going on there. Mrs. Judd stated that her husband had, before the episode in question, never telephoned home merely to ask "What's going on?" And she said he had done so only two more times in the eighteen months that had elapsed since December, 1967. Mr. Judd, on the other hand, thought that he had telephoned home to inquire about what was happening at home as often as once a month. This is an important point in considering the possibility of a chance coincidence between his telephone call and something unusual happening to a member of the family.

A rough calculation of the probability that Mr. Judd would telephone home during any given hour can be made as follows. In order to be more conservative, let us accept Mr. Judd's estimate that he has done this, at least since the particular accident to Celeste, about once a month. Mrs. Judd said there was no particular hour at which he would telephone home more than at other times; he could call at any time of the day. Presumably, however, he would be much less inclined to telephone home within an hour of leaving the house or within an hour of returning to it. We might then suppose that there would be six hours in each working day during twenty-two working days each month when he might telephone home. The odds against his telephoning home within an hour of some injury to a member of the family would thus be about 132 to one.

These are not very high odds and I consider this case of borderline significance with regard to the likelihood that it includes extrasensory perception on the part of Mr. Judd. (He himself, I should add, was quite diffident about it and attached much more value as providing evidence of extrasensory perception to others of their experiences.) I have considered the case worth reporting, however, as an excellent example of the sort of experience that may be due to extrasensory perception, although such experiences are often simply dismissed as "coincidence." It can be seen too, that if Mr. Judd had included only one more detail in his experience, say that Celeste was the person in distress or that the dog had attacked someone at home, the experience would certainly be credited as paranormal. Yet throughout this monograph I am trying to show that some and perhaps many experiences in which the percipient can report nothing but an unexpected change of feeling may be extrasensory perceptions.

This is yet another case in which two persons (here Mrs. Judd and her young daughter, Celeste) might have acted as agents. Mrs. Judd distinctly remembers having thought of her husband immediately after the dog attacked Celeste; we do not know whether Celeste did or did not think of her father at that time.

Case 14

The next case was first told to me by Lieutenant Colonel Howard T. Wright and his wife, Audrey Wright, during a conversation in Bethesda, Maryland, on June 21, 1968. The percipient was Colonel Wright's mother, Mrs. Margaret S. Wright. She is an elderly lady in her eighties and I did not meet her. From notes I made during my interview with Colonel and Mrs. Wright I wrote out a statement of Mrs. Margaret S. Wright's experience and their own knowledge of the related event, which was the death of Mrs. Audrey Wright's grandfather during a trip she and her husband made to the Middle West of the United States.

After filling in some details, Colonel Wright and his wife signed the statement, dated July 25, 1968. They also took it to Mrs. Margaret S. Wright and showed it to her. She read it, agreed with it, and then signed a short statement dated July 26, 1968, saying that the statement accorded with her memory of the experience. The joint statement thus attested was the following:

> We [Colonel and Mrs. Wright] were traveling in the west of
> the United States and during our visit to Iowa the grandfather

of Mrs. Audrey Wright died unexpectedly. This delayed our return from the west to Washington by three days.

Ordinarily our mother and mother-in-law, Mrs. Margaret S. Wright, is extremely concerned when anything delays us from an appointment in which she is concerned. On this particular occasion, however, when we returned to Washington we found that Mrs. Margaret S. Wright was not at all upset by the delay in our return. As soon as we met her she said "I knew you had been delayed because Audrey's grandfather died and you went to the funeral."

Audrey Wright's grandfather was ninety-three years old and known to be frail. He was not, however, expected to die and not thought to be in poor health for a person of his age. In fact, Audrey Wright had not even planned to visit her grandfather on this particular trip west.

There was no normal way known to us in which Mrs. Margaret S. Wright might have learned about the death of Audrey Wright's grandfather before our return to Washington. She was not in touch with his family and was not directly notified of the death by the family of the deceased man.

Mrs. Margaret S. Wright apparently had no visual image of the death or funeral, but just got an impression that Audrey's grandfather had died and that we had attended the funeral.

Mrs. Margaret S. Wright was not particularly close to her daughter-in-law, Mrs. Audrey Wright, but she had been very close to her son, Lieutenant Colonel Howard Wright.

To the best of our recollection this episode occurred several years ago in 1964."

I corresponded with Colonel Wright further on the question of whether his mother might, on other occasions, have referred to the death of Audrey Wright's grandfather. This led to Colonel and Mrs. Wright signing the following statement, dated September 11, 1968: "To the best of our knowledge the occasion we have described after our return from the trip out west in 1964 was the only time Mrs. Margaret S. Wright ever said that Audrey Wright's grandfather had died, and certainly it is the only time she ever said so in our presence."

Mrs. Margaret S. Wright is among those percipients who have

had several experiences suggestive of extrasensory perception, and I have included another of her experiences in Chapter IV (Case 25).

Case 15

The next case, which occurred in 1938, was first reported to me by the percipient's wife, Mrs. Ivan (Evelyn) Melrose (pseudonym) in a letter dated November 6, 1964. In this letter Mrs. Melrose narrated several instances of apparent extrasensory perception on the part of her husband, including the following paragraph:

> One time we were at a football game in Berkeley [California]. My husband got up suddenly in the middle of the game and said we must go home at once as our son had been hurt. When we arrived home our son had shot a B.B. into his thumb and we had to take him to a doctor to have it removed.

Some years later I was in touch with Mrs. Melrose and requested a statement from her husband concerning this particular experience. Mr. Ivan Melrose then wrote me himself in a letter dated August 6, 1968, as follows:

> In answer to your letter I will give a report of my experience. There was an interesting football game in Berkeley which I wanted to attend. My wife and I went. I believe it was the first time we felt we could leave our son alone. We lived about two miles from the stadium and we parked about five long blocks from it. About three minutes before the first half ended I had a strong feeling that my son had been hurt. The half ended and I asked my wife if she wanted a hot dog and she said, "No." I was restless. I went and got one myself, but I couldn't eat it. I told my wife that I thought Tommy had been hurt and I wanted to go home. She agreed to go. I looked at my watch: 2:25 [P.M.]. We went home.
> My son was standing by the back door and seemed all right. I asked him what happened to him and he said, "Nothing." I said, "No, you've been hurt." He then showed me his thumb and said reluctantly that he had been shooting his B.B. gun. His

gun was defective and the B.B.'s fell out. So he was holding them in with his thumb and it [the gun] went off. I took him and had his thumb X-rayed. It showed a B.B. shot in it which we had removed. When I arrived home and he finally (a matter of minutes) showed me his thumb I asked him, "When did it happen?" and he said, "About twenty minutes ago." I figured this was exactly the time I had the feeling he was hurt.

He also told us that when he had the accident he had first thought of me and was afraid I'd be angry. He was about ten years old.

I wrote Mr. Melrose for more details about the nature of his experience, specifically asking if he had himself felt any physical pain and if he had had a visual image of his son when he became aware that his son had been hurt. He replied in a letter dated August 2, 1968, as follows:

> I had no physical pain of any kind, but a terrible restlessness and nervousness. I just had to leave and get to him. I could say with this strong reaction I had, I saw his image. When you go through an experience like this, you think of the person and see them as they are.
>
> This was the only time my son ever hurt himself with a gun.
>
> As regards the date on which my son was hurt, it was the first game of the season at the University of California which was played the last part of September 1938. My son had just had his eleventh birthday the previous month.

If Mr. Melrose's son had just turned eleven this perhaps accounts for his saying in his earlier letter that the boy was ten at the time of the accident.

Mr. Melrose's reply about imagery left me in doubt, so I wrote again asking if a visual image of his son was part of his *initial* experience or if he only *afterwards* visualized his son as he realized he was hurt. Mr. Melrose then replied in a letter dated August 29, 1968, as follows: "In answer to your letter, it is correct that I did not see my son at first when I knew he was injured. In my worry over him I naturally pictured him in my mind, but not in any hurt condition."

I also wrote Mrs. Melrose to ask her whether her husband had any tendency to make incorrect statements about distress or injury to other people they were separated from. She replied in a letter dated July 26, 1968, as follows: ". . . my husband has never said that he knew someone was hurt when the person was not."

Subsequent to the above correspondence I was able to interview Mr. and Mrs. Melrose in Berkeley, California. We went over this experience in detail, as well as some other apparently paranormal experiences Mr. Melrose has had. Mr. Melrose said that he had never left a football game on any other occasion before this episode and Mrs. Melrose said that she had never known her husband to leave any occasion, whether a football game or other, prematurely before or since this episode. Both also stressed how definite Mr. Melrose's conviction about an injury to their son had been. Mr. Melrose said: ". . . it wasn't a general impression that something was wrong. I *knew* something was wrong." And Mrs. Melrose said "When he got up [during the football game] and told me this, he didn't say: 'I think. . . .' He said: 'Tommy has been hurt.' "

After my talk with the Melroses it occurred to me that perhaps they had had some grounds for thinking the boy's B.B. gun was not working well, so I wrote Mrs. Melrose to inquire about this. She replied in a letter dated February 15, 1969, as follows:

> I will answer your question about the B.B. gun incident as accurately as possible. In order to do this, I consulted my son who remembers the incident clearly. It happened almost thirty years ago. As I told you, I was not sure of his age. He says he was at least ten years old. He remembers distinctly that this was the second B.B. gun he had owned and he had had it for at least a year. I have been under the false impression all these years that it was defective and that he was holding his thumb over the end to hold the B.B. in. He told me that the gun was not defective [and] that for some reason he was not loading it in the usual manner, but was putting one B.B. in at a time from the end of the barrel. He did this while it was cocked and it went off. Neither my husband nor I were worried about the gun being defective. I acquired that idea after the event as I

thought the B.B.'s must be falling out if he had his thumb over the end. Furthermore, we didn't know he was playing with it.

Introductory Comments on the Following Six Cases

The six cases to follow are taken from a large variety of apparently paranormal experiences that have occurred since 1947 to Mrs. Eva Hellström of Sweden. Mrs. Hellström founded the Swedish S.P.R. and has been its Hon. Secretary ever since. She knows the importance of careful documentation and provided this for her own experiences in a remarkable, nearly unique way. She kept a diary for about sixteen years in which she made notes of any experience which seemed to her to be one of extrasensory perception. Frequently she has had the notes in her diary read and initialed by someone else who was with her. When she obtained normal knowledge of the related events she noted these in the diary and also, whenever possible, she collected verifying statements, telegrams, newspaper cuttings, or other relevant information. The notes in the diary, together with the verifying material, were then copied into large notebooks in which each experience was organized with all its material as a separate case. English translations of these notebooks have been made and Mrs. Hellström kindly placed these at my disposal.

In order that readers may be quite clear as to just what Mrs. Hellström did in the keeping of her diary and the preparation of the notebooks, I have obtained from her the following signed statement which was also signed by her former secretary, Mrs. B. Warbert:

> In connection with the publication of Dr. Ian Stevenson's monograph on Impression Cases, I wish to make the following statement about the recording of my experiences which seem to include extrasensory perception during the period of time when I kept records of these. During this period, which extended from 1947 to 1963, I noted in handwriting in diary books any experience happening to me which seemed to include an element of extrasensory perception and only those. Often I had these notes in my diary countersigned at the time by a member of my family or a friend, particularly when I thought the experience was in a precognitive form.

Subsequently the material of the diary notebooks, describing the experiences which I thought included extrasensory perception, was copied with typewriting and placed in large loose-leaf notebooks in which were also inserted additional corroborating and verifying information and testimonies. My secretary, Mrs. Britta Warbert, assisted me in the transcriptions and is a witness to the fact that all experiences suggestive of extrasensory perception were included in the new typewritten notebooks. Mrs. Warbert also assisted in the preparation of a similarly complete English translation of the Swedish notebooks.

Most of my experiences included some kind of sensory imagery, but a small number took the form of impressions.

Date: April 8, 1968   s/ *Eva Hellström*

Mrs. Britta Warbert countersigned this statement as correct as follows:

I have studied the above statement and consider it to be absolutely correct.
Date: June 10, 1968   s/ *Britta Warbert*

Mrs. Hellström describes most of her experiences as "visionary, auditory, or dreams," and a number of them corresponded with subsequent events. In addition to studying Mrs. Hellström's notebooks carefully, I have talked with her (and her husband) in Stockholm about her experiences and she and I have corresponded much about various details of them.

Among her numerous experiences of different types, Mrs. Hellström has had twelve experiences of the impression type from which I have drawn six examples which seem to me the best corroborated or documented of the group.

These six impression cases have one thing in common: they were all concerned with two men who had a deep emotional or physical need for her help. The first four were about a Jan Larsson (pseudonym), a professional man whom Mrs. Hellström first met in 1950. He was talented but very neurotic, perhaps owing to a sad and deprived childhood. His father, an alcoholic, died when he was five years old, and as his mother could not provide for four children he was sent to live with a strict and old-fashioned aunt with whom he was very unhappy. He longed desperately for his mother, toward whom he appears to have developed a love-hate attitude. It looks as if in later life Mrs. Hellström came to represent his mother—he once told her that he had had a vision of the two of them together, perfectly happy in another life—and he drove her to a strong though reluctant sense of responsibility for him. Mrs. Hellström remarked, "I have never had such a strong and trying contact with any person." Possibly his demanding attitude could have provided the "emotional fuel" which facilitated telepathic contact. She once told Mrs. Rosalind Heywood verbally that the feeling she describes as "psychic fatigue" was particularly strong when she got impressions about Jan.

The other two impression experiences reported here related to Mrs. Hellström's husband, Professor Bo Hellström.

Case 16

On May 29, 1951, Mrs. Hellström wrote in her diary:

Jan went to his aunt in Jönköping (approximately 300 km. from Stockholm) on May 24th. He seemed healthy, happy and content. I wondered, though, how it would work, thought that if the visit is a success, it will be a real proof that he is in balance again. (He had had psychoanalytic treatment all [during] the winter.)

May 25th passed. On the 26th at lunchtime, I began feeling uneasy. In the afternoon I felt such a terrible psychic fatigue that I stayed in bed all the afternoon. In the evening Bo [Mrs. Hellström's husband, Professor Bo Hellström] and I attended a big festivity so that I had to pull myself together, but we went home at 10 o'clock.

On the 27th, I was in such a state of anxiety that I phoned G.O. (the psychiatrist) to find out if he possibly knew where the aunt was living, which telephone exchange and what number she had. But he didn't know, only that the aunt lived in Jönköping and that her name was Miss Nilson, one of the most common names in Sweden. After a lot of trouble, I found out the number and put through a personal call to Jan. At once when he answered, he began a fictitious conversation; he pretended that the call was from Dr. O. He said among other things: "I am sorry to hear that my friend is worse; then I must break off my holiday here and go home at once. I will be in Stockholm Tuesday by the first train." I said, "Oh, I see, so you can't stand it any longer?"—"No, that's just it."

When he returned, he told me that he had had a terrible row with his aunt on the 26th at lunchtime. The 27th had been unbearable. During the night he had been awake, praying that I should telephone to him. The call came just in time.

It will be noted that Mrs. Hellström did not make her entry in her diary in this case until after she had had normal knowledge of the distress of her friend Jan. Mr. Larsson, however, described the whole experience to Mrs. Astrid Lindquist, who was his landlady for several years, and Mrs. Lindquist kindly furnished a corroborative statement. An English translation of her letter dated March 23, 1964, follows:

During several years from 1950 and onwards Mr. Jan Larsson rented a flat in my house. It was situated on the ground floor just below my own apartment. His windows faced our garden and therefore we chatted quite a lot when he was sunbathing in his window. He also had the habit of borrowing from me everything that he had forgotten to buy. He told me quite a lot about his private affairs.

My friend of many years, Mrs. Eva Hellström, phoned me the other day and asked if I could remember the time when Jan Larsson went to Jönköping to pay a visit to his aunt. I replied that I remembered the episode quite well, specially as I was told about it both by Mrs. Hellström and by Mr. Larsson himself.

Mrs. Hellström had felt a terrible anguish which she felt had to do with Jan Larsson. At last she found out the telephone number of [his] aunt and reached him over the telephone. Jan Larsson had then simulated a conversation which was meant to give the aunt the impression that he had to go back to Stockholm at once, because a friend had taken ill.

He told me that he had been praying all night that Mrs. Hellström would telephone him, and he was very upset about the aunt's behavior in connection with some trifling matter. He was very difficult to deal with. On which day this occurred I do not remember.

Case 17

This case is one of three in this main group of cases which does not have corroboration of the experience from independent persons. Since, however, accounts of both experience and related event were recorded by Mrs. Hellström in her diary promptly (that of the experience being noted down in writing before Mrs. Hellström had any normal knowledge of the related events) I feel justified in counting this case among reasonably well-authenticated ones.

The following extract is taken from Mrs. Hellström's diary of April 28, 1953:

Last night I must have had some dream or other experience, which I don't remember anything about. I only know that I was awakened by saying to myself: "No wonder I felt as I did yesterday."

On Monday, April 27th, the day before this, I felt such terrible anguish—felt quite paralyzed and couldn't undertake anything. I had planned to stay home and do some writing, but had to lie down. I wonder if possibly Jan has been taken ill?

Mrs. Hellström's record of the related event occurs in the diary under date of May 2, 1953:

On May 2nd, I telephoned to Gerard and Mary [Ejvegaard]. They had not . . . heard anything from Jan. I was sure that he had been ill. I sent a telegram to Florence [where Jan had been staying]: "Are you ill?" Sunday morning, May 3rd, he arrived in Stockholm and wanted to see me at once. I went to his flat at 12:30 [P.M.]. He then told me that he had left Florence a week ago, but had got poisoned by food on the train. On the Monday he had been almost unconscious and had been in bed in a room somewhere in Switzerland. That was April 27th, when I had been so beside myself with worry and had had the dream the night after. Then it had taken him a whole week without a sleeper to get back home. Now he was almost well again.

A note in the diary signed by Gerard Ejvegaard testifies that the above "is in accordance with what I remember," thus corroborating Mrs. Hellström's statement that she telephoned to him and his wife on May 2nd to inquire about Jan. Mr. Ejvegaard did not furnish independent confirmation of Jan's illness, but his signed statement in the notebooks furnishes partial corroboration of Mrs. Hellström's experience since she would not have bothered to inquire about Jan if she had not been concerned about him because of her impression.

Case 18

Mrs. Hellström has described how over the years she and her husband had tried to help Mr. Larsson, but eventually this became so difficult that by the time the following experience occurred they had not seen him for nearly a year. The following account is taken from the diary entry of February 16, 1961:

> On February 14 and 15, 1961, I felt that very intense psychical fatigue, which somehow hurts around the thyroid gland. I felt a kind of anguish, but I was too tired to be able to relax so that I could sleep.
>
> On the 15th I said to my husband and to my secretary, Mrs. Warbert: "If it had been a few years ago, I would have considered this fatigue to be telepathy from Jan, but nowadays I never have any personal contact with him, you know."
>
> On the 16th, my husband received a letter from Jan, who was traveling abroad. It concerned the possible publication of a scientific paper, which my husband had written, on a natural scientific explanation about the Israelites' Crossing of the Red Sea. Jan wrote that he thought a Catholic paper would be interested. The letter was written on the 14th when my psychical fatigue [had] begun. We have not had any contact with Jan since April 1960, when we went to see him at the hospital in Copenhagen. He was on that occasion so unfriendly and negative that we decided not to care about him any longer.

Possibly he now felt an inner anxiety when he again tried to get in touch with us.

Mrs. Hellström's husband, Professor Bo Hellström, and her secretary, Mrs. Britta Warbert, wrote of this experience: "That Eva Hellström mentioned her feeling of fatigue and told us as stated above, and that the letter arrived on February 16, 1961, we herewith confirm."

Case 19

The fourth incident of apparent telepathy with Jan Larsson was recorded by Mrs. Hellström in her diary on December 10, 1962:

> When my secretary, Mrs. Warbert, was with me on December 5th, I said to her that I was feeling somewhat tired and depressed . . . the last few days. I wondered if it was because I was taking penicillin and sulphate, or if it had something to do with Jan.
>
> On December 7th a Christmas card arrived from Jan. It was addressed only to me (my husband was not mentioned). On the card there was a new translation of a well-known poem and the translation was made by Jan. The card was posted December 4, 1962, according to the postmark, one of the days when I had been in the above-described state of mind.
>
> The last time we had heard from Jan was on February 15, 1961. On that occasion my husband had a letter from him, and I experienced it beforehand in the same way.[5]

Mrs. Warbert confirmed the details of Mrs. Hellström's report, as follows:

> When I came to write for Mrs. Hellström the last time, she told me about her feeling of depression and tiredness, and mentioned her wonder if it had to do with Jan or with the medicine. When I arrived here this morning she showed me a card from Jan in accordance with the above report, which I herewith certify.

---

[5] See Case 18. Mrs. Hellström had her experience in this case on February 14 and 15, 1961. Her husband received the letter from Jan on February 16th.

Case 20

The next two experiences were related to illnesses of Mrs. Hellström's husband, Professor Bo Hellström. The first was recorded in Mrs. Hellström's diary for October 17, 1955:

Bo and I had been to Egypt since October 5, for his work with the Sadd El Aali dam. We had agreed that if he felt quite fit when we left Egypt for good, I should go to London on my way back home and have a holiday for eight or ten days, to see old friends and old dear places there. (I had lived in London for seven years.) On October 16th we flew to Rome together and stayed overnight there. Bo felt fine and saw me off at the airport early in the morning on Monday the 17th and was waving to me when my plane left for London. One hour later his plane left for Stockholm.

I arrived in London after four and a half hours of non-stop flight. As soon as I was installed at the hotel in London I went to arrange for my driving license, to be able to hire a car during my stay in London. In the afternoon I began feeling uneasy. The feeling became stronger and stronger. I got a feeling that I must go home and that it was wrong that I was in London.

At teatime I went to [the] S.P.R. and had tea with the secretary, Miss Horsell, Mrs. Goldney, and Dr. Soal. Miss Horsell told me that the famous Frenchman, Gabriel Marcel, was going to deliver a "Myers Memorial Lecture" about ten days later, and hoped that I could stay on and attend this, which I very much wanted to do.

My feeling of uneasiness increased, however. The day after, on Tuesday, the 18th, I went [to the airline office] and booked a seat in the first available plane. Wednesday I flew home, without even trying to phone home and inquire. [Mrs. Hellström here omits to say that she did send a telegram to say she was coming home.] I was met at the airport in Stockholm by my eldest son and his wife. They told me that my husband had taken ill in the plane between Rome and Stockholm and was in bed with a high temperature. He had bronchopneumonia. Our daily help, Mrs. Eriksson, had been taken into the hospital for a big operation and had left the flat in a terrible confusion. It was a stroke of luck that I went home. When my telegram came on the Tuesday, that I was coming home Wednesday, my husband had said to my son, Bosse, "I am sure Mother has felt instinctively that I have fallen ill." He had never been happier than when he received my cable that I was coming home.

Professor Hellström made a note in the diary corroborating the above account as according with his recollection of the events. In October 1961 Mrs. Hellström recorded the following additional comment about this experience in her diary:

> I never felt that my husband was ill. I only felt a kind of uneasiness and felt that it was wrong, somehow, that I was in London, and that I must go home. I have been alone in London both before and after this occasion and never had any feeling of worry. And last September I went alone to U.S.A. without any anxiety and everything was well. Only on one other occasion have I had that feeling—see case October 25, 1957 [Case 21].
>
> On Tuesday I sent a telegram home that I was returning on Wednesday.

Case 21

In October (the exact date was omitted in the diary) 1957, Mrs. Hellström recorded a somewhat similar impression that something was wrong at home, on this occasion connecting it definitely with her husband:

> My husband and I had been to a conference in Geneva. I left him there and went alone to a health resort in the Pyrenees, Amélie-les-Bains, where I spent three weeks and had hot swimming baths. When I had been there for some time, I suddenly got a feeling that something was the matter with Bo. I felt anxiety and wrote home that if he wasn't well I could go back home now. After some days, October 25th, I received a telegram saying "Me porte très bien. Bo" [I am very well. Bo] so I stayed on for a time.
>
> When I returned home my daily help, Mrs. Carlsson, told me that my husband on that occasion had been in bed with bronchitis for several days. Surely he had wished that I had been home, but had not wanted to ask me to come home earlier from my cure.

Mrs. Carlsson wrote a corroborating note in the diary. Mrs. Hellström also kept the telegram from her husband, which was included in the documents of the case. In 1961 Professor Hellström added a comment to this experience in his wife's diary and stated that during his illness he had Mrs. Carlsson come in for several hours daily to look after him, so he did not want to bring his wife home. Mrs. Hellström said (in a discussion with Mrs. Rosalind Heywood) that she still thought her husband might subconsciously have felt uneasy at her absence, because some years earlier he had suffered badly from asthma, for which she had learned to give him injections. It will be noted that this slight difference of opinion about Professor Hellström's wishes does not concern Mrs. Hellström's actual experience—which was simply that something was the matter with her husband.

Comment on Mrs. Hellström's cases: As mentioned earlier, the foregoing six impression cases are only half of those recorded by Mrs. Hellström in her diary. Of the twelve, five have independent corroboration and verification, three others are supported by documents or secondhand reports from reliable persons, and the remaining four depend on the entries in Mrs. Hellström's diary. In judging her cases, especially those that are not independently corroborated, it is important to remember that she conscientiously recorded in her diary over a period of sixteen years *every* experience that she thought might be paranormal. In nearly every instance she made her initial diary entry about the experience before she had normal knowledge of the related events. If this is accepted, and I believe from my knowledge of Mrs. Hellström that it should be, then she had twelve impression experiences during this period of sixteen years and was correct as to the person concerned in every instance.

Mrs. Hellström's experiences illustrate particularly well the importance of agent focusing. Examination of the records of these twelve cases shows that in eight of them the agent was known definitely to be thinking of Mrs. Hellström at the time of her experience, and in a ninth (the agent being a very close friend of hers who was dying) it seemed very probable that he was thinking of her. In the other three cases there is no record that the agent was focusing on Mrs. Hellström, although in one of these also it seems rather likely that he was.

Mrs. Hellström's cases also illustrate the tendency, noted in other percipients who have had more than one spontaneous experience, for certain persons to act as agents more often than others. In Mrs. Hellström's twelve impression experiences, her friend Jan Larsson was the agent in nine instances, her husband in two, and a close friend in the other. Similarly, three of Mrs. Joicey Hurth's impression experiences occurred with her daughter, two with her son, and one with her father as agent.

Case 22

The percipient in this case is Mrs. Rosalind Heywood, who has been active in psychical research for many years as an investigator and author. She has also had a large number of paranormal experiences herself and has published a full account of many of them along with much relevant biographical material (21). I know her well and have talked with her about her paranormal experiences, althought not about this particular one.

Mrs. Heywood had the experience about to be described on April 28, 1969; she made a note in her diary about the impression and its verification the same day. She first described the incident to me in a letter dated August 2, 1969, from which I quote the following:

> The first [of two impressions described by Mrs. Heywood in the same letter] was in my bath. I suddenly felt, for no apparent reason, that I must ring up a very busy novelist just to say "How are you?" This seemed illogical as I did not know her very well, had not seen her for a year, and not often before that. . . . A few years before I had been able to be of some slight use to her in standing up to a dominant personality who was asking altogether too much of her.
>
> . . . reluctantly I rang her up, feeling rather foolish because I have great sympathy with writers who are interrupted by telephone calls, especially for no apparent reason. I said, apologetically, that I must ring up to know how she was, and she replied, "Oh, I was thinking of you *so* hard half an hour ago.

I *do* want your help. Can I come and see you?" It was again a problem concerned with the dominant personality and I was also able to be of some slight use about another problem which was worrying her very much. The point of interest here is that I actively did *not* want to ring her or anyone else up, but I felt forced to do so.

I asked Mrs. Heywood if her friend the novelist would furnish a statement about the episode and she obtained for me a statement signed by Mrs. S. Lethbridge (pseudonym). The statement itself is not dated, but the date is fixed by a letter from Mrs. Lethbridge to Mrs. Heywood dated August 18, 1969, which Mrs. Lethbridge sent with her statement. Mrs. Heywood's date for the episode is also (approximately) confirmed in this letter because Mrs. Lethbridge mentioned that she had gone to visit Mrs. Heywood at her home on May 1st, a fact that she noted in her diary. This would be three days after the impression and their telephone conversation. Mrs. Lethbridge's statement follows:

I have much pleasure in confirming Rosalind Heywood's account of our experience of spontaneous telepathic rapport. One morning in late April of this year (1969), during a period of what might be called reverie subsequent to waking, the thought of Rosalind Heywood presented itself sharply and suddenly to my mind. There seemed no speculation or query attached to the image of her: she was just "there"! Though, a moment after, I remembered and thought about our last conversation of (I think) over a year ago, when I had dropped her home in my car after a conference we were both attending. About half an hour later the telephone rang, and I was greatly surprised to hear her voice—yet of course, at the same time, on another level it seemed "only natural." Rosalind Heywood and I are literary colleagues, and on terms of mutual respect and sympathy. Occasionally we ring each other up about something connected with our interest in psychic studies—we very seldom meet—I didn't even know that she had been very unwell. Rosalind Heywood said rather shyly and apologetically that she was obeying a very strong impulse (I think it came to her in her bath?!) to ring me up. I told her that it seemed an incontrovertible example of telepathy between us, and that, far from feeling that she had disturbed me, I was extremely glad to hear from her. I then found myself saying: "As a matter of fact I'm terribly depressed. Can I come and see you?"

I had, in fact, been "in a depression" for several weeks— the cause being anxiety over the mental state and general unhappiness of my fifteen-year-old granddaughter, with whom I have very close links. Directly I had said this [that is, after she had asked if she could visit Mrs. Heywood], the cloud of perplexity seemed to begin to lift. However, I continued at intervals until the next afternoon, when we met, to wonder what on earth had induced me to burst out (very untypically) with a private trouble to someone with whom I had never been on confidential terms.

That afternoon remains memorable to me because of my gratitude to Rosalind Heywood for the insight and sensitivity of her approach to my problems vis-à-vis the child. I realized that we shared the same kind of concern for our children and their children. When I went down a week later to see this child at school I was quite confident of having found the clue to helping her—and so it was!

There is an unimportant discrepancy about the date of Mrs. Lethbridge's visit to Mrs. Heywood. In her statement Mrs. Lethbridge said it occurred "the next afternoon," but in her letter to Mrs. Heywood, written presumably on the same day as the statement, she said she visited Mrs. Heywood on May 1st. Possibly Mrs. Lethbridge did not make her diary notation until two days after the visit which would then later make her erroneously think the visit actually occurred that day.

In Mrs. Heywood's first statement to me about the impression, she did not mention getting any details of Mrs. Lethbridge's condition. But in a letter to me dated September 5, 1969, she said she had found a note in her diary (April 28, 1969) to the effect that she had felt she (Mrs. Lethbridge) was depressed before she telephoned her. Mrs. Lethbridge confirmed in her statement that she was in fact depressed at the time Mrs. Heywood telephoned her. And she had earlier stated this in a letter to Mrs. Heywood dated

May 27, 1969, from which I extract the following: "I feel constant gratitude for your response in my time of strange anxiety and depression."

After receiving Mrs. Heywood's first statement of the impression, I wrote her asking various questions particularly concerning her contacts with Mrs. Lethbridge in personal meetings or by telephone during the period before the impression and telephone conversation of April 28, 1969. Mrs. Heywood stated that she had not met Mrs. Lethbridge personally since the conference they had attended together in 1968. Mrs. Lethbridge said in her statement that this meeting occurred "over a year ago." (Mrs. Heywood stated in her letter of August 15 that she had in her diary a notation of the date of the conference—June 14, 1968.) She and Mrs. Lethbridge agreed that they had not met for (approximately) eleven months before the impression and the meeting it led to. (Mrs. Lethbridge's comments on this and other points to be mentioned were sent to me by Mrs. Heywood with a letter dated September 5, 1969. She met Mrs. Lethbridge on September 4th and they discussed the details of the incident. Mrs. Heywood then wrote a report of this discussion the following day. Mrs. Lethbridge subsequently signed (September 9, 1969) a copy of this report which Mrs. Heywood then forwarded to me.)

Mrs. Heywood and Mrs. Lethbridge both also affirmed that they had had no telephone conversations during the same interval. They said that it was possible there had been a telephone conversation between them, but neither of them could remember any. And Mrs. Heywood was quite certain that she had not previously felt any pressure or urgency to telephone Mrs. Lethbridge as she did on April 28th.

Mrs. Heywood (in her letter of August 15, 1969) furnished the following answers to questions about the experience that I had put to her in one of my letters:

1. The experience was purely impression type. Simply, "I *must* telephone to Mrs. Lethbridge." No elaboration.

2. I had no reason whatever to think she was in any trouble when I telephoned her.

3. I cannot be exact . . . but I should say the interval be-

tween the impression and telephoning was probably less than an hour.

4. Had I thought about Mrs. Lethbridge at other times? As you say, this is an impossible question to answer and I would guess that I had certainly done so vaguely, if only because books by her are on my book shelves and a mutual friend occasionally mentions her. But—I know, of course, that this is not "evidence" —vague thoughts are quite different to what I call—a bad word, but I use it for want of a better—Orders. [Mrs. Heywood has published a fuller description of what she calls Orders and given other valuable examples (21).] *You must do this now. You must take action.* It is hard to explain, but one doesn't know whether to say "*I* must do it," or "*You* must do it." It is, I think, rather a feeling of "That is required of you."

As to whether Mrs. Lethbridge had thought of Mrs. Heywood during the (almost) eleven months during which they did not meet, she stated (to Mrs. Heywood, who forwarded this to me) that she could not guarantee that she had not, but had no recollection of having done so.

Mrs. Lethbridge further stated that on the morning of Mrs. Heywood's call, she felt no special desire to see or hear from her. She experienced, she said, "a picture of her."

Comment on this case: If Mrs. Heywood and Mrs. Lethbridge had (between June 1968 and April 1969) thought of each other or even had a telephone conversation both had subsequently forgotten, it seems quite clear that Mrs. Heywood had not experienced any urgent desire to telephone Mrs. Lethbridge during this interval. That she did so within an hour of an occasion when Mrs. Lethbridge was thinking of her, quite likely for the only time during the same interval, strongly suggests some connection between Mrs. Lethbridge's thought of Mrs. Heywood and Mrs. Heywood's impulse to telephone her. I believe the facts of the case justify considering it another instance of telepathic rapport in which agent focusing was a relevant factor.

Mrs. Heywood was apparently responding to a need on the part of Mrs. Lethbridge. But it is worth noting that Mrs. Lethbridge was not thinking of Mrs. Heywood with a conscious desire for her assistance. In fact, she expressly denied this. And she was rather surprised when she found herself asking Mrs. Heywood if she could visit her to discuss her difficulties. Yet when she was talking on the telephone with Mrs. Heywood, the idea of visiting and talking with her about the difficulties on her mind came to expression quite easily. Mrs. Heywood, because she had helped Mrs. Lethbridge once before, might well have been a person to whom Mrs. Lethbridge could have turned for assistance. But this was not on the surface of her mind when she thought of Mrs. Heywood on the morning of this incident. There are two possibilities to consider. Subconscious portions of Mrs. Lethbridge's mind may have "emitted" calls for help to persons known to have been helpful in the past and Mrs. Heywood "received" the message. Or Mrs. Heywood, subconsciously scanning the environment for persons she might help, may have been drawn to Mrs. Lethbridge as such a person. The first seems the more likely hypothesis and it accounts better for Mrs. Lethbridge having an image of Mrs. Heywood come into her mind at the time. The image came into consciousness, but no awareness (at that moment) that Mrs. Heywood could be helpful in the present situation. It is certain that Mrs. Lethbridge's image of Mrs. Heywood was not generated by Mrs. Heywood being just about to telephone, because Mrs. Lethbridge said she had her image about half an hour before Mrs. Heywood called her.

Case 23

Mrs. Heywood was also the percipient in this case, while her husband, Colonel Frank Heywood, was the agent. In a letter dated August 15, 1969, Mrs. Heywood sent me the following summary of the case which she made from an account written down (on June 18, 1964) shortly after the impression occurred:

> We were on holiday by the sea in Brittany. There were five miles of dunes and after tea he [her husband] used to go out, by car, and practice golf on a flat grassy area to the landward side of the hilly, sandy part which faced the sea. In this hilly part of the dunes I had noticed two holes, which might

have been rabbit holes, but had seen no rabbits, and no holes in the areas where he practiced.

I lay down on my bed, thinking how lovely it was to be idle, no one to telephone, no work to do. About half an hour later, when there was no reason to do so, I began to fuss. "Frank has put his foot in a rabbit hole. He may have sprained his ankle. I ought to go and look for him." I must make it clear that the impression was only of his putting his foot in the hole. The ankle-spraining was my deduction from it.

I got up, very restless, not knowing what to do, whether to go and look for him—he had taken the car and I didn't know to which of his favorite spots he had gone. Finally, with great effort I compromised between my imagination and a bit of me which didn't want to go, by deciding that if he was not in by dinner time I would go.

In fact he came in quite happily as usual for dinner. I said first, "I've been fussing, I thought you'd put your foot in a rabbit hole." He laughed and replied, "I did put my foot in a rabbit hole. And I sent you a message to tell you so." I asked, "What exactly do you mean by that?" "Oh," he said, "Just that I thought of you as I fell." I suspect that the answer here is that as he fell, being an old man, he was frightened of hurting himself and automatically wanted me to come to his help.

After receiving Mrs. Heywood's account of the impression and event I wrote and asked if her husband could corroborate it. Questions that I put to him were answered, signed by him, and returned to me with a letter from Mrs. Heywood dated September 22, 1969. In the following I have modified the wording, but not the sense of the questions, to accord with Colonel Heywood's answers, since the questions were originally phrased in indirect discourse.

Q. Did you put your foot in a rabbit hole when playing golf in Brittany in 1964?

A. Yes.

Q. As you fell, did you think of your wife, Rosalind?

A. Yes.

Q. What was the date, exact or approximate, of this fall?

A. June, 1964.

Q. When you returned to the house where you were staying,

did your wife say to you that you had put your foot in a rabbit
hole before you told her that you had actually done so?

A. Yes.

Q. Had your wife ever told you on any other occasion that
you had put your foot in a rabbit hole?

A. No.

Q. Had you in fact ever put your foot in a rabbit hole on any
other occasion?

A. Not that I can remember.

In amplification of the answer to the last question, Colonel
Heywood said that he naturally could not guarantee that he had
never put his foot in a rabbit hole on some other occasion, but
could not remember ever having done so.

In the letter mentioned above, dated September 22, 1969,
Mrs. Heywood wrote further about the experience as follows:

> From my side, the impression was so strong that I got up
> from bed and walked about the room struggling against the im-
> pulse to go and look for him in case he had sprained his ankle.
>
> I should probably have gone, but as the possible area covered
> about five miles and he had taken the car, I didn't know where
> to begin, on foot!

In reply to a question whether Colonel Heywood had actually
sprained his ankle when he fell into the rabbit hole, Mrs. Heywood
said (in a letter dated October 11, 1969) that he had not. She
added that "it has just now occurred to me that Frank said he
thought of me as he was falling and he may well have *expected*
to damage his ankle and thought of me as coming to rescue him
if he was immobilized."

Comment on this case: In *The Infinite Hive* Mrs. Heywood
gives several other examples of apparent telepathy between herself
and her husband (21). In three of these instances she was the
percipient and in one he was. In addition, Mrs. Heywood has
described in correspondence to me several other occasions when
her husband had been the percipient in apparently paranormal
communications between them.

The present case might seem at first glance to fall into the category of "trivial," and certainly the outcome was "not serious" —to use the phrase I prefer. But when an elderly man begins to fall on an isolated sand dune he does not know whether he may break a bone and perhaps lie helpless and alone for a time until someone happens to come along and give aid. The situation is accordingly one that could generate much anxiety and an automatic plea for help. Looked at this way, the event to which Mrs. Heywood's impression related was not at all trivial, but very similar to most of the other events that have figured in these impression cases.

Concluding Remarks on the Foregoing Twenty-three Cases

The events related to the foregoing impressions were quite unusual. Four of them were deaths, which may be regarded as clearly unique events; and in most of the others the related events were accidents or illnesses of a type that would happen only once or at most only a few times in the lifetime of a person, and so they also could be regarded as distinctly unusual. If the testimony of the percipients and the corroborating witnesses is believed, as it is by me, then there can be no doubt that the percipients had no normal knowledge or means of inferring the related events before having their impressions. In nearly every case there is also clear independent evidence that the percipients recorded or told about their impressions before learning normally of these events.

The remaining point of weakness in such cases is the possibility that the percipients were in the habit of making statements about misfortune to their friends and relatives which then just sometimes turned out to be correct. On this point the somewhat bald statements which I asked the witnesses to sign perhaps do not do justice to my probings in interviews and correspondence. I have made every effort to discover such tendencies in the percipients. There are, of course, public and private prophets who issue long lists of calamities to come. Some of these may have the gifts they claim, although I have the impression that they gain their popular support because they and their followers remember their successes and forget their many failures. However that may be, the percipients in the present cases are not members of this group, so far as I have been able to learn, and I have spared no pains to find this out if I could. Although a number of the percipients have had several experiences of the impression type or other types of extrasensory perceptions, the corroborating witnesses invariably stated that the percipient had never before made a statement (or taken corresponding action) about the related event similar to what he said or did at the time of these experiences. I therefore believe that, with the possible exception of Mr. Judd's experience (Case 13), we can confidently exclude chance as a reasonable explanation for the correspondence between what the percipients said or did and the related events.

Chapter Four

SOME VARIANT CASES OF THE IMPRESSION TYPE, TEN OF THEM HITHERTO UNPUBLISHED

Introductory Remarks

In this section I shall present some cases of the impression type (ten of them hitherto unpublished) which vary somewhat in content from what we may call the "standard" impression case. I refer to cases without apparent agency, cases relating to future events, cases of apparent communication of pain or other physical symptoms, and cases with somewhat different emotional content from the usual cases. Cases of this type seem to me no less important than the more ordinary sort of impression cases and we certainly need to include them in any attempt to understand the whole range of experiences in this general group.

Readers will note that I have admitted into this section some cases lacking the independent corroboration and verification that were obtained for most of the 160 cases analyzed in Chapter II and for most of the twenty-three cases reported in Chapter III. I have obtained such independent support for most of the ten newly-reported cases in this section. As for the previously published cases that I cite, it seems justified to mention them as examples of variant cases of the impression type which should be included in any consideration of the range of experiences of this general category.

Warnings Without Apparent Agency

Under this heading fall cases in which a person becomes aware of some imminent danger which he had no apparent reason to expect or infer. The following two experiences published by Mrs.

Rosalind Heywood are typical of such warnings. The first experience was told to her by the percipient, her husband, who was an artillery officer in the First World War:

> He was working at a forward artillery observation post on a hill top which was being heavily bombarded. Nevertheless, he kept his companion on the job until suddenly, he "knew" that the moment had come. "Now!" he cried. "Drop everything and clear out." They just got away as a shell fell slap on the post (21, p. 108).

For the next experience, Mrs. Heywood was herself the percipient. At the beginning of May 1941, she was standing with Professor Gilbert Murray in Parliament Square when he pointed to the Houses of Parliament and said, "Well, they haven't hit them yet." At this she nearly cried out (but unfortunately for evidence she refrained), "Oh, don't say that!" because at his words she had a sudden impression that they would be hit the following Saturday. Later in the week she had another impression that her husband's club would also be hit that night. As it happened, it was on that night that both the House of Commons and her husband's club received their only direct hits of the war. And, incidentally, it was the only night during the war on which her husband left his bedroom to take shelter, and so saved his life (21, p. 133).

Tyrrell reported still another case of this warning type:

> . . . On 24th May, 1930, Mr. E. G. Eames, a surgeon, was driving his car from St. Albans to London. He was a fast driver, and was in a hurry to reach London, where he had several operations to perform. But a small car, driven in a leisurely manner, in front of him kept him back. There was nothing to prevent him from overtaking the car and passing it, as he would certainly have done on any other occasion; nor was there reason for any apprehension about the car, which was being driven soberly and well. "But on this occasion," he says, "I absolutely could not pass. Some exceedingly strong something insinuated into my subconscious brain that an accident was going to occur. It was definitely a force quite apart from, shall I say, earthly

impressions." A lorry was proceeding just in front of the car which Mr. Eames was following, when suddenly, a stationary car opened its door and blocked the way for the lorry, causing it to stop abruptly. The small car following the lorry crashed into it, and two of the occupants, a child and his mother, were badly cut. Mr. Eames, by being on the spot, was able to attend to the injuries of the mother and child and to take them in his own car to a nearby hospital. . . .

"This [Mr. Eames said] is the third time in my life that I have felt these strong compelling forces or influences warning me of danger, and always I have been afterwards very deeply grateful that I have been forewarned" (75, pp. 75-76).

Lukianowicz reported two similar experiences occurring during German bombardments of England in the Second World War. The percipient reported the first as follows:

Once, during the German bombardment of [our] town, when my parents wanted to go down to our shelter in the garden, something "told" me not to go. I begged my family to keep away from it, and became hysterical . . . The very next minute our shelter received a straight hit by a bomb which completely destroyed it. Afterward everybody cried from excitement (30, p. 325).

The next experience, which took place shortly after the death of the percipient's father, was very similar, and may possibly have been due to his memory of the first:

One day, on our way home, I was caught, together with my mother, by flying bombs. We were rushed into a public shelter by police. At first I stood with a group of people in the center of the shelter, when, again, something told me to get away from this place. I did, and moved to the entrance of the shelter. I asked the others to follow me; but they only laughed and nobody moved, but my mother. After a few seconds a bomb hit the center of the shelter, and only I and my mother, and a few people who stayed near the entrance, remained alive . . . (30, p. 325).

A similar warning impression occurred to Sir Winston Churchill also during the Second World War. For no apparent reason he turned away from the door of his car, which as usual was being held open for him, walked round the car and got in on the other side where he sat during the journey. Shortly afterwards a bomb fell near the car and tipped it up in such a way that it would have rolled over but for the extra weight of Sir Winston's body on the raised side. When asked later why he had changed to the far side of the car, Sir Winston said at first, "I don't know, I don't know." But then he added, "Of course I know. Something said to me 'Stop!' before I reached the car door . . ." He then felt he was being told to open the door on the other side and get in and sit there—and that is what he did (13, p. 161).

J. H. Hyslop reported yet another case of this type which, however, took the form of an auditory warning. A man who was hunting (alone) was about to fire his gun when he heard a voice distinctly say, "Don't shoot." This was repeated three times, but he shot anyway and was badly injured in the face by the explosion of his gun which had been defective, although fired without incident just shortly before the percipient heard the warning voice (25).

Case 24

In January, 1962, I learned of a further experience of this type during a conversation with a friend and colleague, Dr. Jerrold Hammond, then a child psychiatrist at the University of Virginia School of Medicine. At the time of his experience Dr. Hammond was an American army officer stationed in Europe during the Second World War. After my talk with Dr. Hammond, I wrote down an account of what he had told me and submitted it to him. He changed a few details and signed it as according with his own memory of the incident (January 15, 1962). The report follows:

> During the Second World War, I was in London at the time of the bombardment of the city by German rockets of the V-1 type. These rockets came over the city with motors making a rather loud noise until they cut off before the bomb dropped.

After a little experience with these bombs it became possible to judge accurately how far away they were. If one considered a bomb near, there was usually time to take shelter; if the bomb seemed distant one did not bother to take shelter. At the time of the following incident I had had about six months experience in judging how near the bombs were to me.

On one occasion I heard a bomb above the city and judged it to be quite distant. From previous experience I would say that it seemed to be about three miles away from the hotel where I was staying. But as I listened to the bomb from my bed where I was lying, I suddenly had an extremely strong impulse to take cover. This seemed quite irrational, but I yielded to it and went into the bedroom's cupboard. A moment later the bomb fell, but instead of falling at a distance, fell very close to the hotel. The blast blew in the windows; and the room and the bed where I had lain a few minutes before were sprayed with flying glass and other debris thrown about by the blast. Also the bed clothes were penetrated by shreds of glass.

Other than the sense of imminent danger, there was no imagery or content associated with the impulse to take cover. The experience did not include anything like a warning voice. This was the only occasion on which a bomb fell as close to me as the one of this incident. All other bombs I heard fell a considerable distance farther away from me. Also this was the only occasion on which I ever had such a strong impulse to take shelter from one.

This experience happened in approximately January or February of 1945.

Discussion of Warning Cases

Cases of this kind present two puzzles: how are they to be evaluated and how, if they do contain an element of extrasensory perception, does the information get to the percipient?

The simplest explanation for such cases, especially those which include falling bombs, might be some kind of retrospective falsification of memory. A person who wished to account for the seeming miracle of his sudden escape from death might attribute this to a hunch that in fact he had never had. This explanation may well apply to some cases, especially those in which we have only the percipient's word that he took cover on those occasions and no others. Nevertheless, there does seem reason to believe that on certain occasions, some persons who were not in the habit of ducking bombs, did have a special hunch to do so which was afterwards justified. This would seem to be the case with Sir Winston Churchill and Dr. Hammond, and I believe it probable in some other instances as well.

But if the hunches did have some paranormal sources, what were they? There was no obvious human agency. Were they then due either to a clairvoyant power combined with a computer-like ability to calculate at great speed when and where the relevant bomb would fall, or to some discarnate agency, or to a subconscious relation to time of which, consciously, we are unaware? The available cases of this type are far too few to estimate such possibilities and I include them here chiefly in the hope that other investigators will note, report, and analyze larger numbers of them.

IMPRESSIONS RELATED TO FUTURE EVENTS

So far in this monograph I have reviewed and reported cases in which the events related to the perception were either clearly contemporaneous with it or at least in the making at the time of the perception, as would be the case presumably with falling bombs. Impression cases related to definitely future events do occur, however, and judging by L. E. Rhine's collection of unauthenticated cases, perhaps quite commonly. In a series of 3290 spontaneous cases of mixed types she assigned 258 to the group of precognitive impressions (48). Precognitive impressions thus formed about 7.8 per cent of the total collection of 3290 cases. There were 1066 precognitive cases with imagery. There were 943 impression cases of both contemporaneous and precognitive types in this series and precognitive cases formed 27.3 per cent of the impression cases group. In a later analysis of a larger number of similar cases, Rhine found that precognitive impressions formed 31 per cent of the impression cases (50).

In answering questions concerning the case for which her mother was percipient (Case 2), Miss Alice Langley mentioned in passing an occasion when she and her mother had both responded to an urgent impression that they should return home. They found that this was appropriate for a severe illness requiring an operation which Miss Langley developed two days after they returned home. Some subliminal awareness of her own developing illness might have accounted for Miss Langley's impression, but not so readily for that of her mother. And there certainly are precognitive impression cases that cannot be accounted for easily by explanations along normal lines.

A typical case of this type was reported many years ago in *Journal* S.P.R. A mother urgently removed her child from a field below an embankment where a train shortly afterwards ran off the track. It fell down the embankment and would certainly have killed the child if her mother had not taken her away (52).

The following cases from my own collection illustrate this type of experience:

Case 25

The percipient in this case, Mrs. Margaret S. Wright, was also the percipient in Case 14. As in that case, I first heard of this experience during an interview with her son and daughter-in-law, Lieutenant Colonel Howard T. Wright and his wife, Mrs. Audrey Wright. As in the other case, I wrote out from my notes a statement concerning the experience which Colonel and Mrs. Wright then studied and signed on July 25, 1968. They then took the statement to Mrs. Margaret S. Wright, who read it and signed on July 26th a statement saying that it accorded with her memory of the experience and related circumstances. The first statement follows:

> On September the 24th, 1967, Lieutenant Colonel Howard Wright was bitten by several yellow jackets in his garden in Bethesda, Maryland, at about 6:00 P.M. Subsequently he was taken to Sibley Memorial Hospital in Washington, D.C., and treated for a dangerous anaphylactic shock. The following report concerns the behavior of Colonel Wright's mother, Mrs. Margaret S. Wright, in connection with this episode.
>
> At about 5:00 P.M. on Sunday, September the 24th, Mrs. Wright telephoned her daughter-in-law to ask how her son, Howard, was. At this time, Colonel Wright had not yet been stung by the yellow jackets. Mrs. Audrey Wright was some-

what surprised at the telephone call and inquiry from her mother-in-law. So far as she knew, her husband was and had been entirely well since his recovery from an illness about two months earlier. To satisfy her mother-in-law she looked out of the window and saw that her husband was well and working happily in the garden. She reassured her mother-in-law as best she could and the telephone conversation ended.

Shortly after this telephone conversation Colonel Wright was bitten by yellow jackets [had a severe, near fatal reaction, and was] rushed to the hospital. [This occurred between 5:30 and 6 P.M.] Mrs. Audrey Wright was herself taken up with trying to find out about her husband and help him, if she could, during the crisis of his shock and treatment. She [therefore] did not telephone or see her mother-in-law, Mrs. Margaret S. Wright, until the following morning.

The next morning, September the 25th, Mrs. Audrey Wright went to see her mother-in-law early. Her mother-in-law immediately asked her what the trouble had been and Mrs. Audrey Wright then told her about her husband's serious illness of the night before. Mrs. Margaret S. Wright then said that she had been apprehensive for three days before the yellow jacket stinging about the welfare of her son, Colonel Wright. Her tension concerning his health had built up until she had made the telephone call at 5:00 P.M. on Sunday, September the 24th. The attempted reassurance of her daughter-in-law had not in fact reassured her and she had remained agitated and had slept little all that night.

Mrs. Margaret S. Wright is close to her son and does like to keep in touch with him. She did not, however, have any tendency to call up to inquire about his health unless she had some normal reason for knowing that he was in poor health. And during the six weeks preceding the stings and shock of September the 24th, Colonel Wright had enjoyed excellent health following the recovery from the illness which he had had in July and August.

Case 26

For the next case the informant is Mr. A. Lilieberg of Stockholm. He initially wrote out an account of the case for Mrs. Eva Hellström, who transmitted it to me. Mr. Lilieberg's account follows:

During the 1920's I and my little family used to spend our summers in Norway, staying with an elderly Norwegian deaconess, Edla Rosen, a relative of my wife.

The summer [of] 1928 we intended to go over to Norway as usual. . . . The journey was to go by train to Duved in Jamtland and from there by car over the Swedish-Norwegian border Alps to the place of destination. First my wife and my little five-year-old daughter were to go and I was to join them in a week.

The departure was settled for Thursday June 21st by the night-express to the north of Norrland with time for departure 7:00 [P.M.]. The tickets for the sleeper were fetched, a big trunk had been sent off a few days in advance and all other luggage was almost packed and ready.

Wednesday, June 20th, in the morning a telegram arrived from Norway sent from the little village [of] Rora in Verdalen on June 19th, late at night as was later confirmed. The telegram said: "Come Saturday instead reply Edla."

On receiving the telegram we thought that our old friend and driver, Sverre Hofstad, who always used to meet us at Duved, had been prevented from coming to meet us on Friday. I cabled an answer to Hofstad that he could meet us Saturday June 23rd.

The tickets were changed to hold good for departure on June 22nd by the night express.

In the morning of June 22nd all newspapers announced that a terrible railway disaster had occurred during the night, just outside Bollnäs where the night express to the upper part of Norrland had collided with an engine. Many killed and wounded.

The carriages which were destined for Ostersund and Storlien were the first in the train. They were to be switched over to another rail at Bracke from the carriages destined for Riksgransen. These four were to take the impact and amongst them the sleeper was totally destroyed. My wife and the little girl went on June 22nd as was agreed with Hofstad. After a week I joined the family.

Later when we asked Aunt Edla about the reason for her telegram, she answered: "Dear children, I do not know why, but I was overcome by such a disheartening feeling sitting in Rora in the evening of the 19th that you must not travel by that train, so I simply had to send you a message."

The percipient in this case, Miss Edla Rosen, is deceased. Mr. Lilieberg furnished a photostatic copy of the telegram she sent dated June 19th. He also sent a copy of a portion of the newspaper *Dagens Nyheter* dated June 23, 1928, which contained a full account of the railway accident in which at least six persons lost their lives.

In response to inquiries from me, Mr. Lilieberg answered two questions (translated by Mrs. Eva Hellström) as follows:

Q. Did Aunt Edla at any other time send telegrams advising delays in travel or give other similar warnings which were or were not confirmed by later events?

A. Aunt Edla, who was religious, would, according to her own statement, on isolated occasions feel a certain inner uneasiness in connection with some coming event, about which she couldn't know anything, for instance the big landslide at Verdal, Norway, 1893. At that time she was about thirty years old and lived in Verdal. She has told that she felt a strong restlessness the evening before the landslide. This is perhaps not so remarkable as it is said in a published account about this catastrophe which I have, that even horses [in the area] had been very restless some time in advance of the slide.

Q. Did bad weather in any way contribute to the railway accident? (A storm going on for a couple of days might have impeded visibility and also made an accident more predictable on rational grounds.)

A. Any influence by the state of the weather is quite out of the question as far as the Bollnäs catastrophe is concerned. During the period good summer weather prevailed both on the Norwegian and the Swedish side. In this case the human factor comes into the picture. The driver of one of the engines had simply misunderstood the given order.

The above answer still left me in some doubt as to whether Aunt Edla had ever warned the family about railway accidents before the episode of the present case. I therefore wrote again and received through Mrs. Hellström a statement from Mr. Lilieberg, dated October 7, 1968, as follows: "In reply to Professor Stevenson's letter to Mrs. Eva Hellström, I should like to add to my last report on the railway disaster at Bollnäs that my Aunt Edla never on any other occasion sent us a telegram advising a delay in travel."

Case 27

For this case the percipient and sole informant is Mrs. Maude Stradling of Philadelphia, Pennsylvania. The experience occurred in (approximately) 1951. Mrs. Stradling first described it to me in a letter dated September 26, 1961, as follows:

> Our family had not lived in the neighborhood very long, so there were no close friends that I knew. Also at that time of my life I was a bit withdrawn. On one side [of the area where she lived] there was a walkway to go through to the front street (which is a shopping area) and the walkway was also for the convenience of the shop owners to use their [back doors]. A young couple used this entrance quite regularly, always parking their station wagon in front of our home. The girl was pregnant, I noticed, but what was so strange to me from the very first time they used the walk [was that] a feeling came over me —one feeling was a compassion for the woman with child and the other fear that this handsome man (her husband) was going to hurt the young woman.
>
> I made an inquiry about them (I had become concerned), heard they were not long married, much in love and the girl's mother owned the dress [shop] in front. A baby boy was born not many weeks after and the proud dad brought both home to the maternal grandmother (using the walk same as always). Six weeks later I awoke between 12 midnight and 1 A.M. with sounds of screaming and heard faintly "kill-murder." I ran to the back window and saw the figure of a man running away toward the front of the walkway. It was the handsome man and the story came out next day that he had beaten his wife and six-weeks-old son quite severely—and that was the end of my strange feeling.

In 1968 I took up the study of this case again and corresponded further with Mrs. Stradling about it. It seemed to me that Mrs. Stradling might have had more acquaintance with the man who beat his wife than I had understood, or that she might have picked up information about him in the neighborhood which would have led to a reasonable inference that he was a man given to violence. In reply to my inquiries, Mrs. Stradling replied in a letter dated July 12, 1968, as follows: "Now about those people, they were complete strangers to me, and a feeling came over me when they would pass by. . . . The first time the couple walked past me, I received the impression, and I had never seen them before. I made an inquiry as to who they were because of the impression, but did not tell anyone."

Thinking that perhaps Mrs. Stradling had heard some gossip about the young couple which stimulated her impression, I wrote again on this point. She replied in a letter dated September 10, 1968: "In the case of the young couple, there was no gossip, as we were new to the neighborhood and no one contacted me . . ."

As Mrs. Stradling wrote, she kept her impression to herself (until after the occurrence of the related event) and so it cannot be corroborated. So far as she could tell, the couple seemed to be happily married and gave no outward indications of the trouble ahead which registered with her consciously. From her testimony, therefore, it seems unlikely that she had gained any normal knowledge which could have led to a rational inference about the man's later conduct. The case, however, lacks independent corroboration and verification of the related event.

In December, 1969, I had an interview with Mrs. Stradling in Philadelphia and discussed further details of the experience with her. She emphasized that her unpleasant awareness of impending trouble for the young couple lasted for about two months; i.e., from the time toward the end of the wife's pregnancy when she first saw the couple until the baby was about six weeks old. The subjective state was a "heavy feeling" that was definitely unpleasant for her. She said her impression of impending trouble increased on the night the husband actually beat his wife and child. Mrs. Stradling remembered that she moved to her window to see if anything was happening. (However, in her letter of September 26, 1961, quoted above, she said that she was awakened "with sounds of screaming" and then went to her window and saw the man running away.)

In addition to the fact that Mrs. Stradling's impression related to a future rather than a contemporaneous event, the case is unusual in two other features. The impression related to strangers and the theme was the aggressive action of one of the possible agents toward the other. I shall comment later, in citing a few examples, on the comparative rarity with which impression experiences are concerned with hostility on the part of the agent, at least toward the percipient. In the present case the hostility detected in Mrs. Stradling's impression was directed toward the wife of one of the possible agents, the wife herself being the other possible agent.

Mrs. Stradling has had a number of other apparently paranormal experiences. Once she had an impression that her daughter had injured herself and was in a hospital at a time when her daughter had in fact cut her foot and had been taken to a hospital for necessary suturing of the wound. Mrs. Stradling was in Philadelphia and her daughter on the New Jersey coast when this episode occurred. On another occasion, Mrs. Stradling had an imaged experience the details of which corresponded closely with those of an automobile accident her mother was in at the same time. On this occasion Mrs. Stradling's mother was in Kentucky while she was in Philadelphia. Most of Mrs. Stradling's apparently paranormal experiences concerned members of her family—her mother, daughter, and brothers—but she has had some other experiences, in addition to the present one, that concerned strangers.

Case 28

The percipient in this case was Mrs. W. K. Schlotterbeck, of Dallas, Texas, who first wrote me about the experience in a letter dated February 19, 1969. The relevant portion of the letter follows:

> I think it was around 1950 that my husband left on a business trip from Philadelphia to Boston, and then was planning on going from Boston to Washington by plane. (He went by train to Boston.) After he left I told a friend of mine, who was at the house when he left, that I had a feeling I would not see him alive again—that I felt he should not take the plane from Boston to Washington. I could hardly wait until the next day to call him. When I got in touch with him I begged him not to take a plane to Washington. It turned out that he did not have to go to

Washington after all, and he returned to Philadelphia a few days later. I thought no more about my intuition until he told me that he had reservations on a plane, but cancelled at the last minute. That is the plane that was flying from Boston to Washington, and crashed into the Potomac, killing all aboard. The exact date of it can be found in *Life* magazine, as there was a big write-up about the crash.

My husband, who is a regional manager of a large electric company, has always traveled . . . and very often by plane—so it was not because it would have been unusual for him to go by plane.

At the bottom of Mrs. Schlotterbeck's letter was a statement signed by her husband, Mr. W. K. Schlotterbeck, as follows:

I will corroborate the above statement in that my wife did call me and tell me not to take a plane from Boston to Washington. And I had a reservation on the plane that crashed into the Potomac, but cancelled the reservation at the last minute, because of no need to go to Washington.

In reply to questions put by me, I received a further letter jointly signed by Mr. and Mrs. Schlotterbeck in which they stated first, that Mrs. Schlotterbeck had never on any other occasion advised her husband against taking a flight from Boston to Washington or, for that matter, between any other two cities; and secondly, that Mr. Schlotterbeck himself had not experienced any uneasiness about taking an airplane on this particular occasion.

Mrs. Schlotterbeck also added the following in response to my request for a more precise specification of the airplane crash they were referring to:

My husband seems to think it was around October, 1949. It was no later than December, 1950. We do know that it was piloted by a Bolivian pilot who was in the U.S. training. The plane crashed into the Potomac and all aboard [were] killed. *Life* magazine had a big write-up on it and showed the pictures of all who had been killed. My husband thinks it might possibly have been Eastern Airlines.

This further information enabled me to apply to the National Transportation Safety Board for a list of air carrier accidents in the period indicated. From this list I made a preliminary identification of the airplane crash and confirmed it with details published in the *New York Times* of November 2, 1949. On November 1st, a Bolivian pilot training in Washington had ignored (or not heard) directions from the flight tower of the Washington National Airport and his plane struck an Eastern Airlines plane that was approaching the airport to land. The Bolivian pilot miraculously escaped, but the Eastern Airlines plane fell into the Potomac River and an adjoining lagoon. All aboard were killed or died soon after the crash. The Eastern Airlines plane, a DC-4, was flying from Boston (with a stop in New York) to Washington, and was then due to go on to New Orleans. (Mrs. Schlotterbeck was correct in saying that a Bolivian pilot was involved in the accident, but wrong in assigning him to the plane on which her husband had been scheduled to fly.)

Subsequent to the above correspondence with the National Transportation Safety Board, I had a long interview in Dallas with Mrs. Schlotterbeck. We reviewed her apparently paranormal experiences, including the present one, and I also spent some time with Mr. Schlotterbeck discussing his recollection of the occasion. The following further details came out during the interview:

Mr. Schlotterbeck was only away from their home (at that time in Philadelphia) for about three days altogether. Mrs. Schlotterbeck became uneasy about his flying almost as soon as he had left. She told her friend about her concern the next day, but could not reach her husband to ask him not to fly until the evening before the flight, i.e., October 31, 1949. She reached her husband at about 9:00 P.M. that night. On the telephone he told her he would not fly, but in fact he still intended to do so. About an hour later he received an unexpected telephone call from his associates in Washington telling him of a change in plans which no longer required him to go to Washington. Mr. Schlotterbeck then cancelled his ticket on the morning flight from Boston and hurriedly took the night train for Philadelphia, which he reached the next morning.

I asked Mr. Schlotterbeck if he had any records that would document the fact that he was booked to travel on the plane that crashed and not on some other flight. He replied that he had not preserved any such records, but he and his wife said that they were both quite certain that he had in fact a reservation on the flight that ended in the crash in Washington. And presumably if this had not been the case, there would have been no special reason for them to have remembered Mrs. Schlotterbeck's unusual request to her husband, or they would have remembered her as having been wrong in her impression.

COMMUNICATION OF PAIN OR OTHER PHYSICAL SYMPTOMS

The literature of psychosomatic medicine contains many instances of one person taking on, through identification, a pain originally experienced by another with whom he had a strong emotional bond. The syndrome of couvade in which a man imitates the symptoms of his wife's labor pains and delivery has been well documented with numerous examples (73).

I once studied a middle-aged woman who complained of severe pain in her right shoulder for which physical examinations could discover no cause. Eventually I learned that shortly before her illness began, her son had died of cancer of the gall bladder, and that irritation of the diaphragmatic nerves had referred the pain induced by the cancer to his right shoulder. I have reported elsewhere another case of pain occurring through identification with another person (68).

Patients with schizophrenia are particularly inclined to assume, and genuinely feel, the emotions and physical pains of the persons around them. Searles has described the case of a female patient who complained of pain in her knees which she related to her nurse's difficulty in walking the previous week. The following notes were made by the nurse about this episode:

> [She] called me to rub her back. Says she has my knees.
> "Why, Ruth?"
> "Because my knees hurt."
> "How did you know my knees hurt, Ruth?"

"Last week you walked funny and this week you don't."
I told her that was because I was wearing my arch supports.
"I'm glad for you, but every time you get a new body, they give me your old one, and you change bodies so often" (60, p. 260).

The appearance of stigmata in persons of a certain type of religious temperament provides further examples of the taking-on of physical changes and symptoms by a person emotionally attached to the sufferer (72, p. 123).

Pain due to identification and mediated normally through the senses raises the question whether a similar identification can take place by means of extrasensory perception. This possibility was considered and put to experimental test by psychical researchers of the nineteenth century. Barrett, Gurney, and others reported experiments on the extrasensory communication of pains and tastes from agents to hypnotized subjects (2).

A considerable number of spontaneous cases also testify to the phenomenon. So far I have myself collected only a few cases of this type, but other investigators have published a number of examples and I am inclined to think that the experience is rather common. L. E. Rhine has reported a considerable number of cases of this type in her collection of unauthenticated spontaneous experiences (51). In a collection of approximately ten thousand such cases she assigned 169 (1.7 per cent) to this group. Since these cases lack corroboration (or verification of the reported related events), one cannot say how many of them include paranormal processes.

Excellent examples of this type of case were reported in *Phantasms of the Living*. One concerned a well-known landscape painter, Arthur Severn, who went out for a sail early one morning while his wife was still asleep. She was awakened later, about 7 A.M., by a blow on her lip so violent that she sat up and looked for blood, but, to her surprise, found none. When her husband returned later on for breakfast he was holding his handkerchief to his lips. He explained that they had been gashed, he thought about 7 A.M., when the tiller of his boat swung over in a gust of wind and hit him in the mouth (18, pp. 188-189).

L. E. Rhine has reported a somewhat similar (but uncorroborated) case in which the percipient suddenly "doubled over, clutching her chest as if in severe pain and said, 'Something has happened to Nell, she has been hurt.' " Two hours later the sheriff arrived to tell that Nell had died on the way to the hospital. She had had an automobile accident in which a portion of broken steering wheel had pierced her chest (49, p. 107).

Heywood published another case of the type in some detail, with supporting testimony. A woman in Israel gave birth to a premature baby over five weeks before the expected date. On the day of her delivery, this woman's mother, who lived in London, experienced severe "stomach pains" lasting about three and a half hours. She did not locate them more exactly, but described them as "almost unbearable." She had no normal knowledge that her daughter had gone into labor that day, or any reason to expect a premature birth. Her pains came on first about the time her daughter's labor had ended, so the peaks of discomfort did not correspond exactly (20).

L. E. Rhine also reported a case similar to the foregoing. Again, the mother of a pregnant woman experienced pains in her back at the same time as her daughter, in another community, went through an unexpectedly premature labor and delivery. This case contained the interesting detail that the mother (percipient) had severe pain throughout an entire night, whereas her daughter and presumed agent had no pain at all during her labor and delivery. The case therefore suggests that the mother had some paranormal awareness of her daughter's labor, but had added to this an hallucinatory experience of what she expected her daughter to be going through (49, pp. 106-107).

In his autobiography C. G. Jung described a personal experience of physical sensation apparently mediated by extrasensory perception. He had helped a man out of a severe depression for which the patient had been very grateful. Shortly thereafter the patient had married, and his wife was jealous of Jung's influence over him. Jung had told him to return for further treatment should he ever feel any signs of renewed depression, but fear of his wife's disapproval prevented the patient from doing so, and

Jung had heard nothing from or about him for some time when he had the following experience:

> At that time I had to give a lecture. . . . Around midnight I returned to my hotel, after having had something to eat with some friends, and went immediately to bed. But I stayed awake a long time. At about two o'clock—I must actually have been asleep—I woke up with terror and was convinced that someone had come into the room. It seemed to me also as if the door had been rapidly opened. I immediately put on a light, but there was nothing there. I thought someone had mistakenly opened the door, and I looked up and down the hall outside, but everything was quite still. "That's strange," I thought, "it certainly seemed as if someone had entered the room." Then I tried to think back, and it seemed that I had been awakened with a dull pain as if something had struck against my forehead and then had pushed against the back of my skull. The next day, I received a telegram saying that this patient had killed himself. He had shot himself. Later I learned that the bullet had lodged at the back of his skull (27, p. 143).[1]

Another case of this type was sent to the A.S.P.R. by the percipient.[2] A short account of it was published by Rush (54). The percipient reported:

> My daughter was away at college . . . and I started to write to her as usual; when I had about finished, my right hand started to burn so I couldn't hold the pen and the pain was terrific . . . Less than an hour later we received a telephone call from the college telling us our daughter's right hand had been severely burned in the laboratory with acid at the same time I felt the burn . . . (54, pp. 18-19).

Dale reported a case in which the percipient awakened from sleep with an intense pain in the right arm and hand. She thought she had been dreaming, but could not remember the dream before she went back to sleep again. Later when she again awoke

---

[1] Translated from the German by me.
[2] The original letter is on file at the A.S.P.R.

she recalled that she had been dreaming of her son who was then a few hundred miles away at college. She then mentioned the dream to her family. "In my dream," she reported, "I had seen him walking toward me, and I had remarked that he had looked different for some reason." The percipient's account then continued:

> Late the next afternoon when I returned home from downtown, I found that my son had come home unexpectedly. I called him, and as he came walking down the stairs, the first thing I noticed was his bandaged right hand. My experience of the night before was brought home very vividly. He had been in an accident and his hand had been very badly cut. On comparing notes, we found that the time element was the same as in the dream (6, pp. 34-35).

The percipient's daughter wrote a note corroborating the fact that her mother had told the family about the dream at breakfast and that her brother had suffered an injury to his hand and arm corresponding in location and time of occurrence with the details of their mother's dream. The percipient had no known reason in her own health to have experienced pain in her arm at that time and she had only dreamed of her son once or twice in the year preceding this particular experience.

W. F. Prince reported the following experience in a lengthy series of spontaneous cases. The presumed agent (and the initiator of the report of the case) was a professor of mathematics at an American university. He wrote: "My sister [name and address given] has told me of having a distinct premonition . . . of a severe automobile accident to my wife and myself in France in 1922. You might write to her. I consider any statement from her as reliable."

Prince, accordingly, wrote to the writer's sister and received the following reply:

> On May 30, 1922, I awoke earlier than usual (about 6:30 A.M.) and, not wishing to disturb my husband who was sleeping, went into another room to dress. Walking about twenty feet down

the hall, as I stepped into another room, a blow seemed to strike the back of my head, so affecting me that I staggered, grasping the door to keep myself from falling. In a short time I returned to the bedroom, finding that the noise had awakened my husband, who asked, "What is wrong?" I replied, "A strange thing, I felt as though I were struck on the head, and am sure something terrible has happened to —" (my brother). Mr. — replied, "You were probably faint, lie down until you are better." It might be mentioned that I have always been subject to fainting, but this was nothing of that sort; for when I left my room I was perfectly well. At the time I did not mention the matter to my daughter, but felt very depressed, and so was not surprised when, at about 11:30, the cablegram came announcing the serious accident to my brother and his wife. My daughter told me [that] as I read it, I said, "I am not surprised, for I expected it." Allowing for the difference in time between France and the United States, we think that this peculiar circumstance occurred at the time of the accident.

My brother and his wife were motoring out to the battle-fields when the car struck a tree. My sister-in-law received injuries from which she never recovered; my brother, aside from an injury to the knee, was struck on the head, the result being a slight concussion, and they were both in the hospital at Chalons-sur-Marne all summer.

Mr. — [her husband] died in 1926, but my daughter well remembers the incident which, upon receipt of the cablegram, I related to her (44, pp. 268-269; case 140 of Tabulation).

Cases of this kind are not confined to the apparent transmission of pain; in some instances other kinds of physical symptoms and physical illnesses seem to be at least initiated by means of extrasensory communication. Obviously, extrasensory perception need not be the most important factor in such illnesses, but it might perhaps be the precipitating one in an illness already prepared by other causes.

Schwarz reported eight cases of this type which he investigated (59). His cases include instances of illnesses precipitated by stress undergone by another person emotionally related to the percipient, but who did not in fact have the symptoms or illness of the percipient; and instances in which both percipient and agent did have the same or similar symptoms.

Fourteen of the percipients in the cases analyzed in Chapter II of this monograph experienced physical symptoms. One of them actually had an attack of jaundice reportedly related to his impression. Four other percipients were so distressed and apparently physically unwell that they thought *they* were dying, when in fact the agent was dying (three cases) or ill (one case).

Osty described the experience of a sensitive who developed symptoms of liver disease immediately after he had handled an object belonging to a man who had liver disease and about whom he (the medium) had given veridical information (40). The symptoms lasted about ten days. This could not be a case of transferred infectious hepatitis if, as reported, the sensitive developed his symptoms immediately on giving his "reading"; however, more details about both illnesses would have been desirable. Tenhaeff has described similar instances of sensitives "taking on" the physical symptoms of persons with whom they were in telepathic contact (71).

Eisenbud has reported the case of a woman who, after many years of freedom from asthma, developed an attack on the actual day when her son, unknown to her, was killed in France during the Second World War (12).

Heywood reported another case in which she herself was the percipient:

> While getting the breakfast I unexpectedly felt so very ill and depleted that the idea struck me, "Well, I'm growing old, perhaps I'm going to die." Then I thought muzzily, "At least I'd better try and get Frank's [her husband] breakfast first," and somehow carried on. A few minutes later my husband came down in his dressing gown, flopped on to a chair and confessed, rather shamefacedly, that he had nearly fainted as a result of too long and too hot a bath. He had never done this before (21, p. 109).

The following cases from my own collection provide examples of this type of experience.

Case 29

The percipient in this case, which occurred in 1959, is Mrs. Joicey Acker Hurth, two of whose experiences (Cases 11 and 12) I have already described in Chapter III. Mrs. Hurth wrote out for me an account of another experience in which she had felt physical pain in relation to an injury of her daughter, who was then at school. Mrs. Hurth's account, which accompanied a letter to me dated May 24, 1967, follows:

> The children had left for school and the house was quiet. I was busy in the kitchen of my home at 273 E. Portland Avenue, Cedarburg, Wisconsin, when suddenly I felt a sharp pain on the lower side of my right leg and buttocks. Although alone I said aloud, "Oh!" and rubbed the area where I had felt pain. I glanced at the clock but went on about my usual housekeeping business. When the children came home from school at lunchtime I asked if anything unusual had happened about 10:30 that morning. My daughter said, "Yes, a boy ran into me with his bike. It hit me right on my backside and I hollered, 'Oh!' " She rubbed the spot where she had been hit and the location was identical with the place on my own body where I had felt pain that morning. It was recess time at the Cedarburg Elementary School when the incident occurred in 1959. The injury was slight. The impression which I had received was more startling than profound and I had no image of what had happened, only a feeling.

The agent for this experience, Joicey L. Hurth, Mrs. Hurth's daughter, sent me her own account of the episode in a letter dated April 19, 1967, from which I extract the following:

> The incident referred to . . . occurred when I was quite young. I do, however, remember it well as I was very surprised at [my mother's] reaction to my experience of slight pain. I was playing on the grade school playground when another child ran into my backside with his bike. I jumped, said "Oh!" I rubbed the spot. When I came home that afternoon my mother asked me if anything had happened to me at that time. When I told her, I was particularly amazed by two things—one, she felt a pain,

said "Oh," and rubbed herself, and two, she thought of me at the time and associated her physical feelings with me.

I believe there is a communication between my mother and me. Often I have called to tell her where I was. On the spur of the moment I would know she was worried and my call would relieve her anxiousness.

I then wrote Joicey L. Hurth for further details and she sent replies to my questions dated May 25, 1967, as follows:

Q. How old were you when this happened?

A. I was ten years old and in the 4th grade at Cedarburg Elementary School, Cedarburg, Wisconsin.

Q. Had your mother on any other occasions said that she had thought of you and experienced pain in her bottom?

A. No, although she had on occasions felt pain in sympathy with some pain I had (such as toothache, earache, etc.).

Q. When you and your mother exchanged remarks about your being hit by the bike, did you tell her what had happened to you first or did she tell you that she had felt a pain in her bottom and thought of you first?

A. When I returned from school my mother asked me if anything happened at approximately 10:30 A.M.; I then related the experience to her.

Q. Has another child ever run into you with his bike on any other occasion?

A. Yes, as a small child of three, a boy hit me with his bike. I was taken directly home, only a block away.

Q. If so, did he hit you in the same place?

A. No.

Since Joicey Hurth said her mother had thought of her at the time she (Mrs. Hurth) felt the pain in her leg and buttocks, I wrote Mrs. Hurth to inquire about whether imagery had entered into her experience. In a letter dated September 18, 1968, she replied as follows:

> To answer your questions regarding the time my daughter was hit by a bicycle: To the best of my recollection I was acutely conscious of only two things: (1) pain in my own leg

and buttocks, and (2) the time, because I deliberately looked at the clock in front of me. I did not associate the pain with Joicey at the precise time I felt the pain. No, I did not have a visual image of Joicey being hit. I did not at the time realize what caused the pain I felt. It was my own questioning of my children later that revealed the incident of my daughter being hit by the bicycle, which proved to be at the exact time that I felt the pain (her recess period at school).

As mentioned earlier (Case 12), on another occasion Mrs. Hurth not only had a paranormal impression that Joicey (specifically identified) had been hurt, but knew she had been hit by an automobile. On the present occasion, however, Mrs. Hurth (contrary to Joicey's memory of what she said) did not, at least immediately, relate her impression to Joicey.

Case 30

This case was first described to me during an interview I had in Charlottesville on October 29, 1968, with the percipient, Mrs. Dora Martin,[3] and her twin sister, Mrs. Martha Morrison. They have had a number of experiences in which one or the other of them apparently had paranormal knowledge of something happening to the other one in another community.

I will introduce the case by quoting first a portion of the transcription of the tape recording of the interview I had with the two sisters. As they had previously told me briefly about the experience, the interview began by my asking them to narrate it again in full detail. The relevant portions of the interview transcript follow:

Dora: I woke up in Naples, Italy, with pain in my chest and a terrible feeling of depression as if someone had put a cloak over my shoulders. And I could barely . . . and started to cry . . . and I could barely get up and do anything at all. I just didn't want to be bothered. I felt very, very ill. And my husband [a physician] examined me and he said, "I don't think you're sick. You may be coming down with something, but I don't see anything." And

---

[3] Pseudonyms are used for the names of all persons in this case.

so I just stayed in bed for about three or four hours and then the feeling passed. I got up and I felt fine for the rest of the day. And that evening we were talking about this strange awakening, feeling so ill and in terrible pain. I felt like I had a collapsed lung and a . . .

I.S.: Let me ask you a question on that. For the previous, say, month or two you had been entirely well?

Dora: Yes, no problems at all.

I.S.: And had you ever had a pain in your chest like that before?

Dora: No. I felt like the air was slipping away from me. I felt like someone was taking the air out of my lungs and so that evening my husband said, "Well, maybe something is wrong with your sister. We have not heard from her in a long time and you know she's pregnant." So I said it may be. Then ten days later I received a letter from my father telling me that my sister had had a severe pregnancy and severe delivery. The baby was transverse and placenta previa and she had gone into shock and into . . . with such blood loss . . . into coma and that she was unconscious for about four hours during that period of time and when we were talking about it later, it was the period of time practically by clockwork across the ocean that I had awakened with the pain.

I.S.: Now what time of the day did you wake up with the pain?

Dora: About 7:00 in the morning.

I.S.: Did you have the pain when you woke up or did you get it after you woke up?

Dora: I woke up with it.

I.S.: So 7 A.M. And now, Martha, you were in Wayne, Pennsylvania?

Martha: Yes.

I.S.: And what was happening to you?

Martha: That morning I had awakened . . . with an abnormal bleeding. My husband had rushed me to the hospital and they had told me what was happening and that they would have to perform a Caesarean and then things went from worse to much worse. And the baby presented her arm and it was too late for a Caesarean section, so they had to deliver her normally in a matter of a few minutes. . . . When I came out of the anesthesia around 2:00 that afternoon, I developed blood clots throughout my body, localizing in my lungs. And they did not find this out for about ten days . . . that these embolisms had formed from the delivery, but I woke up with the inability to get my breath or breathe or . . . and since I had such a terrible delivery, they blamed it on the delivery itself, never dreaming about the embolisms in my lungs.

I.S.: The embolisms came after the delivery?

Martha: After the delivery, after the vitamin K [which I had been given] had settled.

I.S.: How long after?

Martha: I don't know when they started forming and neither do they.

I.S.: But, I mean, was it the next day?

Martha: No, the delivery was in the A.M. and it was by the afternoon that I could not breathe.

I.S.: Dora, apparently your husband on the day that you felt the pain—he suggested somewhat later a connection. . . .

Dora: Yes, because he couldn't find anything wrong with me. You know, I said "Oh, I'm coming down with an awful flu" and the tears were running down my face. And I told you that I hadn't cried in nine years, but the tears were running down my face and I said "It's just terrible, terrible."

In the remarks transcribed above, Mrs. Martha Morrison did not mention pain in her chest as a prominent symptom after she came out of the anesthetic following her delivery. She had, however, mentioned chest pain at other times, and in a written statement dated June 30, 1969, she stated: "My chest felt like one charley-horse after another, stabbing in the front and coming out the back under the left wing and giving me difficulty in breathing."

After the above interview I wrote to the percipient's husband, Dr. Geoffrey Martin, to ask if he could corroborate his wife's statement about having an unusual pain when in Naples, Italy, at the time of her sister's delivery. In a letter dated January 12, 1969, Dr. Martin replied as follows:

I shall be happy to verify the episode you mention that occurred in Naples.

Dora awoke one morning with a vague pain in the right upper quadrant [of the abdomen] that persisted the whole day.[4] The pain, as I recall, was accompanied by no other [physical] signs or symptoms and did not recur after it subsided. Some time later, we learned that her twin, Martha, had a pulmonary embolus involving her right middle or lower lobe. The timing of the incident is unknown to us, but [we] do know that it was sometime in October, 1959. At the time we became aware of Dora's sister's diagnosis I remember that we were able to place Dora's pain on the same day as the embolus and we ascribed her symptoms to the coincidence.

Since Mrs. Martin had said that she had experienced pain in her chest that corresponded to chest pain experienced by her twin sister, I wrote Dr. Martin to ask if he recalled more exactly the site of pain complained about by his wife. In a letter dated February 5, 1969, he replied as follows:

Dora awoke with pain and I recall that it was in the right upper quadrant [of the abdomen]. Dora had the pain and I must surrender to her recollection. I did, however, feel that gall bladder [disease] was definitely a possible cause and so there must have been some radiation or character [of the pain] that made me feel that way. After that, as we reconstructed the dates and times, they coincided very well with the problem Martha had—and I was told that this was a pulmonary embolus.

The question arose whether Mrs. Martin had experienced similar pains on other occasions perhaps related to disease within herself. She had denied (in the interview cited earlier) ever having had a similar pain, but I put the question to her husband also. As a physician, he would have been a particularly competent witness of his wife's health. He replied in a letter dated February 17, 1969, as follows: "In October of 1959 Dora was not ill nor had

---

[4] The percipient, however, stated that she felt well again a few hours after the onset of the pain.

she been for months before or after the episode of pain. Furthermore, the episode was unusual in that it not only involved discomfort, but also a feeling of depression and anxiety, which was foreign to her normal outlook on life."

In the remainder of his letter, Dr. Martin mentioned that his wife had experienced some acute pain in her abdomen in 1955 and this had been attributed to spinal nerve root irritation. In 1961 she had had some upper abdominal pain that was attributed to spasms of the duodenum. Dr. Martin added, "Dora is not a complainer, but has a rather high tolerance to pain."

Dr. Martin said in his letter that he did not remember the exact date of his wife's pain experience in Naples, Italy. He remembered that they afterwards ascertained that it coincided with Martha's delivery in Philadelphia. In the interview from which I have already quoted extracts, Mrs. Martin said:

> . . . We did not know about this tie-up at all until I received a letter from Dad that she [Martha] had delivered this day and Geoffrey said, "Well, that's the time you kept telling me about this pain in your chest and this terrible feeling of depression."
> . . . I really felt as if someone . . . the only way I can describe it . . . put a black cloak over me. . . .

In reply to a question from me as to how she recalled the date of her experience, Mrs. Martin said (in the same interview): "Because her baby was delivered October 17th and because we had gone to Rome the week-end before, October 10th, etc. And this was the next week-end, I mean the next Monday a week later, so it was the same day or one day [later]."

October 10 and 17, 1959, fell on Saturdays, so Mrs. Martin was correct about the dates being on week-ends, but possibly wrong about having her pain experience on a Monday. Before considering this point further, however, I shall present information I obtained concerning Mrs. Morrison's delivery and accompanying complications.

Mrs. Morrison was delivered on October 17, 1959, at a hospital in Philadelphia from which I obtained confirmation of this fact and xerographic copies of the hospital records. These provided information about some details of her admission to the hospital. Unfortunately, the hospital records were extremely scanty. The labor lasted just a few minutes less than five hours, a long period for a delivery after the first one. The baby was misplaced for delivery and had to be rotated and extracted before delivery. The placenta also was out of the usual position. There was an extensive loss of blood. The attending doctor's notes mentioned no other complications such as pulmonary emboli, but the order sheet showed that a strong analgesic was ordered after the delivery suggesting that pain was anticipated or that the patient had complained of it.

Mr. Edward Morrison, the agent's husband, kindly furnished a statement of what he remembered about his wife's condition after this delivery. His statement dated April 23, 1969, follows:

> I was present in the [hospital] when my wife was delivered of a baby on October 17, 1959. The delivery was extremely complicated and when the obstetrician emerged from the delivery room to talk with me in the waiting room he was very disturbed emotionally and said that my wife and child had had an extremely difficult time. He said that she had had during the delivery severe bleeding on the delivery table.
>
> When I was able to see my wife later that day she was extremely weak and depleted. I do not remember her complaining of any pain, but she was so weak and exhausted that she probably could not complain of anything. She was having difficulty breathing. As nearly as I can recall, I was able to see her about one-half hour after the delivery was over.
>
> Following this delivery my wife remained unwell for some time, complaining of faintness and of pain going from the front of her chest to the back. These symptoms were apparently a residue of the complicated delivery of October, 1959.

Mrs. Morrison had said (in our interview) that her delivery occurred three weeks before term and the hospital records confirmed that the birth was "premature" without saying how early it was. This point is relevant to Mrs. Martin's statement that she knew nothing about her sister's condition and apparently she had no reason to expect her sister to deliver at the time she did; nor had she any reason to expect that her sister's pregnancy or delivery would be complicated. A note in the hospital records states that Mrs. Morrison had complained of low back pain about a month before her delivery, but this site of pain was considerably removed from the areas of the chest in which both Mrs. Martin and Mrs. Morrison say they experienced pain around the time of Mrs. Morrison's delivery.

Mrs. Morrison also arranged for me to receive some notes made by her physician in Philadelphia toward the end of 1960, that is, about a year after the delivery in question. The notes state that Mrs. Morrison was then complaining of having had chest pains since October or November 1959 and a diagram indicated the site of pain as in the left chest. The physician's notes stated: ". . . traumatic delivery of third child, a daughter (1959) . . . shortly after this delivery developed onset of symptoms of chest pain. . . ."

These notes made by the physician a year after Mrs. Morrison's delivery are not contemporary records of what she experienced at the time of that delivery, but they are evidence that she was stating in 1960 that she had had chest pain from about October 1959 up to the time of the physician's examination. Mrs. Morrison says that she was told afterwards that she had had pulmonary emboli and her brother-in-law, himself a physician, was evidently satisfied at the time that she had had such emboli. These would certainly have caused difficulty in breathing and pain in the chest. Although it has not been possible for me to find contemporary documentation of this diagnosis, the available medical records are entirely harmonious with it and I believe it is the correct explanation of the symptoms she complained of after her delivery.

I shall return now to the coincidence of times between Mrs. Martin's experience in Naples, Italy, and Mrs. Morrison's in Philadelphia. Mrs. Martin and her husband were not certain of the exact date of Mrs. Martin's experience, but remembered a general coincidence. Both agreed that Mrs. Martin's experience was first noted by them when she awoke in the morning at about 7:00

A.M. Naples time, which would be 1.00 A.M. Philadelphia time. Mrs. Morrison's delivery was over by 10:00 A.M. (Philadelphia time) and she regained consciousness and became aware of difficulty in breathing not long afterwards. (This was noted by her husband who saw her soon after the delivery.) Mrs. Morrison stated that "it was by the afternoon that I could not breathe." If she had her most extreme discomfort after 2:00 P. M. (as she stated in the interview), this would mean after 8:00 P.M. Naples time. I am inclined to suppose therefore that Mrs. Martin developed her experience of pain and difficulty in breathing during the night of October 17-18 in Naples and that she became fully aware of this and communicated it to her husband the following morning. There may then have been a latent period in this case between the agent's distress and the percipient's awareness of symptoms corresponding to it.

It remains to comment on the correspondence in actual symptoms between the experiences of the sisters. Mrs. Morrison emphasized difficulty in breathing in her account, but said also that she had had considerable chest pain after the delivery. Mrs. Martin, on the other hand, emphasized the pain in her account, but remembered also difficulty in breathing and much depression of mood. These differences in reported symptoms in the sisters may have arisen from differently altered memories of the actual symptoms as they occurred. Or the symptoms may have occurred with the differences the sisters reported, the differences then being due to different physical susceptibilities in response to stress in the two sisters. I believe a rich ore of valuable medical knowledge can be mined when cases of this type are studied contemporaneously and with full consideration of the possibility of extrasensory communication as a factor in the production of physical symptoms.

Case 31

The next case was first reported to me by the percipient, Mrs. Lola Bolles, in a letter dated February 23, 1968. Mrs. Bolles had written me about some recurrent dreams she had had as a child and subsequently which seemed to relate to previous lives. One of these concerned a shipwreck which she saw vividly in the dream.

It is this recurrent dream to which she refers in the beginning of the extract from her letter which follows:

> In World War I, I had it [the dream of the shipwreck] very often but I associated it then with the sinking of boats by the U-boats.
>
> When my husband [an officer in the American army] was to go overseas in 1917 I had the dreams all the time. He was at camp in the East and did not tell me when he was scheduled to leave. [Mrs. Bolles was living in the Middle West at the time.] One night when I lay down in bed, it seemed as if the bed was riding a wave and I became seasick. I was at my mother's so ran to her room and told her that Lem [her husband] had sailed that night. She asked if he had phoned and I told her what had happened.
>
> The next day I wrote him and told him I knew he was on the ocean. He had left several letters for me with a friend, to be mailed so I would not have the gap. When he got mine in France, he wrote and said: "You were correct. I sailed Dec. 13th. How did you know?" All that week the shipwreck dreams were as vivid as though I saw them [the wrecks] close at hand.

Subsequent to receiving this letter I visited Mrs. Bolles, on June 21, 1968, in Washington, D. C., where she resides, and discussed her various experiences with her.

In this interview Mrs. Bolles told me that during her experience when she lay down on the bed, she felt the motion of the waves "just as plain as if I was on the ship." If she stood up, the sensation passed off and returned when she lay down again.

She told her mother that she did not think her husband was to have been sent overseas so soon. She made a note of the date at the time and later wrote the date to her husband in the letter mentioned in her letter to me. She had kept her husband's confirmatory letter about the date of her experience and of his voyage, but unfortunately had mislaid it at the time of my visit.

Colonel Bolles was not seasick during his voyage to France in 1917. Thus Mrs. Bolles' sensation of being seasick herself was part of her reaction to the sensation of motion of the waves and not a communication of the degree of discomfort experienced by her husband on the moving ship.

Significance of Cases of Communication of Pain or other
Physical Symptoms

It seems quite possible that many experiences of the paranormal communication of pain or other physical symptoms occur and fail to attract the attention they deserve or be properly interpreted. If the possibility of such communication is not thought of, the etiological role of paranormal processes as at least precipitating factors in the percipient's illness will be overlooked.

As the foregoing cases show, the percipient's physical symptoms may imitate or resemble those of the agent, or the agent's distress may simply precipitate a physical disorder in the percipient which the agent does not share at all. The factors causing the first type of reaction in some persons and the second type in other persons need careful investigation. One can suppose that ease of identification would facilitate the first type. It will be remembered, for example, that Mrs. Hurth sometimes felt a pain experienced by her children when she knew about it normally as well as in the apparently paranormal experience described in Case 29.

One of Schwarz's cases provides a good illustration of the possible precipitation of symptoms in a person already ill (but not yet symptomatically so) by extrasensory communication. A woman of fifty-six who had stopped regular menstrual bleeding eight years earlier had three episodes of uterine bleeding each associated with the unexpected labors or threatened abortions in her two daughters. The percipient's daughters were living miles away and she was out of touch with them at least as to any information about the unexpected deliveries and abortions which they experienced. Subsequently the percipient had a massive uterine hemorrhage and was found to have a uterine carcinoma twenty months after the last episode of isolated bleeding. It is possible that this carcinoma was already in a nascent state at the time of the three bleeding episodes, each of which was touched off by the obstetrical difficulties of her daughters (59, p. 602).

It seems quite likely to me that many instances of symptoms induced by extrasensory processes are overlooked because this possibility is simply not envisaged. Medlicott reported a case which I cite not as an instance in which extrasensory perception must have occurred, but as one in which it *might* have occurred and in which this possibility could have been investigated at the time if it had been considered. Medlicott's first report of the case was as follows:

> He [a twenty-seven-year-old patient] was very close to his wife and claimed that he would suffer pain in both time and site with her even when they were apart and without ordinary knowledge that she was suffering. During the birth of their son he went through a typical couvade experience followed later by afterpain when his wife had an unexpected episode of uterine colic in the maternity home" (32, p. 675).

In response to an inquiry from me about further details of this patient, Dr. Medlicott wrote:

> He maintained that he had been developing pains whenever his wife did, and that they tested it once [when] she had a severe pain below her knee, said nothing to him about it, and when he returned from work he described this pain coming on at the same time. It also disappeared with hers. He had felt quite ill when he took his wife into the maternity home for the baby; he was having abdominal pains and couldn't sleep that night. He had pains associated with weakness the night following the labor. . . . It must be remembered that what he told me was in no way verified.

Dr. Medlicott's patient was a covert transvestite, his dressing in women's clothing being a further expression of his extreme identification with them. But this strong identification with women in general and his wife in particular may have facilitated communication of physical symptoms through extrasensory perception. Unfortunately, lack of details in this case precludes judgment about whether any of his symptoms contained a paranormal component. It is mentioned here merely to suggest that if the case had been thoroughly studied with extrasensory perception in mind, clearer evidence as to such a possibility might have been obtained. There may well be more such cases which deserve similar study.

It is worth pointing out that if a person sensitive to paranormal communications and liable to their expression in the form of pain or other physical symptoms has repeated episodes of such symptoms having no other obvious genesis, the patient may be unjustly suspected of being hypochondriacal. This seems to me one more reason for at least considering the possibility that a paranormal process may be a precipitating factor in the onset of otherwise obscure physical illnesses.

COMMUNICATION OF FEELINGS AND INTENTIONS OF HOSTILITY AND DECEPTION

In what I have called the "standard" impression case, as illustrated by the examples presented in Chapters II and III, the percipient becomes aware that someone he (usually) loves is in trouble and needs help. The communication takes the manifest form of an appeal for help to a suitable person. It is perhaps surprising that we do not find more examples in which other kinds of emotional relationships occur and other kinds of contents are communicated. Why, for example, do we not find more evidence of the communication of strong hostile feelings and intentions?

One reason may be that such experiences would be more difficult to verify since the people concerned would not have the friendly relationship usually necessary for the exchange of information which could lead to verification of the case. A second reason could be that hostile feelings and intentions may be discharged, so to speak, but not received by the target person because of defenses which protect us from such assaults.

There are, nevertheless, a small number of examples known to me in which the communication of hostile feelings and intentions does seem to have been communicated paranormally. I think, for example, of Abraham Lincoln's dream of his imminent assassination (28, pp. 113-119). That, however, was an imaged perception and we are concerned here with impression experiences.

Case 27, in which Mrs. Stradling was the percipient, illustrates the communication of hostile intentions in the form of an impression, although in her experience the hostile intentions were not directed toward her.

The following are two published examples, taken from *Proc. S.P.R.* The first case included a warning of danger:

> Four years ago, I made arrangements with my nephew, John W. Parsons, to go to my office after supper to investigate a case. We walked along together, both fully determined to go up into the office, but just as I stepped upon the door sill of the drug store, in which my office was situated, some invisible influence stopped me instantly. I was much surprised, felt like I was almost dazed, the influence was so strong, almost like a blow, I felt like I could not make another step. I said to my nephew, "John, I do not feel like going into the office now, you go and read Flint and Aitkin on the subject." He went, lighted the lamp, took off his hat, and just as he was reaching for a book the report of a large pistol was heard. The ball entered the window near where he was standing, passed near to and over his head, struck the wall and fell to the floor. Had I been standing where he was, I would have been killed, as I am much taller than he. The pistol was fired by a man who had an old grudge against me, and had secreted himself in a vacant house near by to assassinate me.
>
> This impression was unlike any that I ever had before. All my former impressions were slow in their development, grew stronger and stronger, until the maximum was reached. I did not feel that I was in any danger, and could not understand what the strong impression meant. The fellow was drunk, had been drinking for two weeks. If my system had been in a different condition—I had just eaten supper—I think I would have received along with the impression some knowledge of the character of the danger, and would have prevented my nephew from going into the office (36, pp. 459-460).

This experience was corroborated by the percipient's nephew both as to his uncle's hesitation to enter the shop and as to the fortunate escape from the assassin's bullet. I did not, however, include it among the cases analyzed in Chapter II because the evidence of paranormal processes seemed questionable. The percipient had no impression of trouble or danger when he was away from the office, in contrast to the "robbery" cases described below in which the percipients sensed that something was wrong at home or shop when they were away from them. When the percipient of this case reached his office, the assassin was close by and possibly some sound made by the assassin might have alerted him normally to a danger. Nevertheless, I feel justified in citing the case here as an example of a type that is rarely reported and may occur more often than is known.

The second example is the following, unfortunately a second-hand report:

> At the close of the Civil War, a northern gentleman with a partner established a mercantile business in a Virginia city. After being there several months, he awoke from sleep in the middle of the night with the thought impressed upon his mind, "There is something wrong at the store and I must go and see about it." He could not account for his vivid impression, for his sleep had been sound and undisturbed by dreams; but obeying the summons he called up his partner, and together they hastened to the place, just in season to prevent their money from being carried off by a burglar (3, pp. 33-34; case 47 of Tabulation).

Prince reported another case in which a percipient seems to have become paranormally aware of a burglary of her house (42, pp. 251-255; case 106 of Tabulation). Hodgson reported another example. In this case a woman while at her dressmaker's became aware that her father's store was being robbed; this turned out to be true when she went there to verify her impression (24). (This case was not included in the analysis in Chapter II because another case of the same percipient was used.)

That hostile feelings may be communicated by extrasensory perception has often been claimed by paranoid persons. They believe that other persons are more hostile toward them than these persons are, or at any rate admit. And they often claim that the hostile feelings of others act on them by paranormal processes so that they can never escape from them. Formal tests of mentally ill persons have not shown that they have a higher than average capacity for extrasensory perception. But formal tests never rule out the possibility that a person may have paranormal experiences under other conditions more suitable for their manifestation. Ehrenwald made the suggestion some years ago that there may be an element of truth in the contentions of paranoid persons (10). Perhaps they do pick up paranormally the hostile attitudes of other persons. The patient's sensitive awareness and excessive reaction to such perceptions might then lead to a sort of reverberation of negative emotions between him and the agents which could contribute to the patient's illness, although it would not be a primary cause of it.

Cases of this sort lend some support also to the considerable (although largely still anecdotal) literature of "voodoo death" (1, 5, 53). Schmeidler has contributed some additional support from a card-guessing experiment she conducted (58) in which she arranged for agents to wish their percipients to do well or to do badly without the percipients knowing which attitude the agents adopted. The results appear to have been affected by the agents' changes of attitude. Fodor suggested that parapsychologists should pay more attention to the extrasensory communication of hostile attitudes (15), and Tanagras has published a number of cases in which hostile feelings seem to have manifested in unpleasant effects for other persons (70).

I believe that if psychiatrists would think more often of the possibility of paranormal influences on their patients they might account for some otherwise inexplicable changes in their patients' condition. I shall cite an example of the sort of situation in which such an influence might be considered. In this particular case there were definite possibilities for normal communication between my patient (the possible percipient) and the presumptive agents. I shall not therefore dignify this example with a separate case number, but I do think it illustrates the type of situation I am describing.

The patient was a forty-five-year-old professor who had become depressed and required admission to the hospital. Disagreements with colleagues in his department had been important factors contributing to his depression. He was not my regular patient, but I took care of him for several weeks during the absence of his own psychiatrist. He was on medication, but it was not changed during this period of observation. Nor did any other circumstances of the routine of his life on the ward or other aspects of his life change during the same period, so far as I could tell.

The patient's course seemed to be even, with a slight tendency toward improvement, when one day he became definitely much worse and complained of this change in his feelings. It turned out later that this worsening of his condition coincided temporally with meetings of his opponents in his department who were, in effect, plotting to oust him from his position.

During the period of my observation of the patient he had been well enough so that he did some teaching while in the hospital. His graduate students used to visit him there for tutorials and seminars. These students knew a little of the patient's difficulties with his colleagues, although they did not discuss these with him during the period preceding the change in his condition. But it is possible that the patient picked up from casual remarks made by his students some information about the hostile intentions of his colleagues. Extrasensory perception may have stimulated the patient's relapse, but cannot be asserted as the cause of this because of the possibility for normal, if subliminal, communication from the students.

Before leaving the topic of the extrasensory communication of negative or hostile emotions, I shall just draw attention to the not infrequent paranormal awareness in some percipients of dishonesty or deception in the persons around them. I have already mentioned the two occasions when Mrs. Hurth became paranormally aware that her young son was doing something of which she disapproved. In one of these instances he was clearly disobeying her instructions, in the other merely doing something dangerous of which she would not have approved. Cases of this kind lend some support to the rather common claims of intuition about another person's dishonesty. Such claims and their supporting evidence deserve much more thorough study than they have so far received.

COMMUNICATION OF FEELINGS AND THOUGHTS OF
REASSURANCE, LOVE, AND HEALING

We seem to have even fewer instances of the paranormal communication of loving feelings or even of good news than we have of the communication of hostile feelings. The occasions for the communication of good tidings such as of birth and weddings or even of material successes are presumably as numerous as occasions of sadness and distress. Is it a failing of human beings that they do not more often communicate news of such happy events by means of extrasensory processes? Or is it that the communication of joy has no survival value for us, while the communication of distress has? Taking only the feeling of the percipient as an index of the nature of the communication, Sannwald found that the percipient reported a positive affect or emotional state in only fifteen per cent of the spontaneous cases in his series, and a negative affect in eighty-five per cent (56,57). This type of communication nevertheless does seem to occur occasionally, as the following examples will show.

An early example of the type, quite uncorroborated but interesting nevertheless, was mentioned by Mme Guyon in her autobiography. She, a most saintly woman, was the apparent agent in the experiences which she described as follows:

Often from the plenitude which filled my soul, I was favored with a freedom to impart or communicate to my best disposed children to our mutual joy and comfort, not only when present, but often when absent. I even felt it to flow from me into their souls. When they wrote to me they informed me that at such times they had received abundant infusions of divine grace. Our Lord had given me that spirit of truth which knows how to refuse the evil and choose the good (19, p. 384).

Coming to more recent times, Heywood reported an uncorroborated case in which a mother became aware (at a rather precise time) of her son's success in an important examination. The perception of this good news coincided in time not with the moment when the son heard of his success, but with the moment a few hours later when he was sharing the news with his older brother (22, p. 239).

Among the cases I have analyzed in Chapter II, there were several "arrival" cases. We may consider arrivals as generally (although not always!) good news. There is also an example in which a woman became paranormally aware, according to the testimony, of a man's intention to propose marriage to her. Unfortunately, the lady's feelings accompanying this impression are not included in the report. We therefore do not know if she reacted to the news with pleasure or otherwise, but we can at least assume that the transmitted intention of the agent was benign and friendly (61, pp. 104-107; case 67 of Tabulation).

An experience of this type was reported at length by Hodgson. (I did not include it in the analysis in Chapter II because it involved a considerable amount of tactile and auditory imagery.) The case is well corroborated and the related facts adequately verified by the agent, the percipient's husband, General John C. Frémont. He had gone on a long and hazardous expedition across the still largely unmapped Rocky Mountains in the winter of 1853-54. He had been on such expeditions before and had suffered from starvation and other stresses, so there was nothing remarkable in the fact that for much of the time her husband was away his wife, who was living in Washington, D.C., was severely worried and indeed wasting away with lack of sleep and appetite.

More remarkable was Mrs. Frémont's quite sudden impression of relief to her husband. After having this impression, Mrs. Frémont fell into a profound sleep from which she awoke much recovered from her previous weakness. News eventually reached her (and her husband later confirmed the facts) to the effect that at the time of her impression of relief to her husband, he had in fact (after a long period of near starvation and other suffering) brought his party into a settlement where they were fed, warmed, and put to comfortable rest. Mrs. Frémont's experience coincided quite closely with the time when General Frémont, having seen the rest of his party taken care of, sat down to rest and write in his journal. And at that moment he wished that somehow "Mrs. Frémont could only know that all danger was past and that it was well with me" (23).

Wickes reported another example of this type of experience, unfortunately without corroboration, but presumably adequately noted by her as she heard of it from the agent, who was in psychotherapy with her. This woman had been possessively attached to her son, ostensibly living her life in sacrifice for his needs, but actually binding him unwisely to her and also denying herself opportunities to develop in other ways. I quote from Wickes' report of the case:

> Summer came and she [the patient] was leaving town. It was her last hour of analysis before fall. As the hour drew toward a close, there came to her like the breaking of a new dawn, a consciousness of her own separate life, a gift originally given, an individual potential which was hers to live whatever might happen in the life of another. She said: "I am going to take up my own life and learn to live it even if I never see him [her son] again. My sorrow will go with me always but it will be my own life that I shall live." It was the end of the hour. The clock struck twelve.
>
> Three days later she received a letter. Its date was the day of her decision. It read: "Dear Mother, I am sitting on a hillside three thousand miles away. Just now I heard the clock strike nine and suddenly I felt that a fear that had been with me always was gone. I am coming home."
>
> The striking of twelve had occurred simultaneously with the striking of nine in the far away village. It was at the moment of her decision that the fear of her enveloping love fell from him (83, pp. 261-262).

These last two cases in which a communication of "I'm all right" occurs may also be examples of a type commoner than is recognized. Still another example is a case in which the percipient had a feeling of "dismal wretchedness" one day. Then he received a telegram from home telling him of the serious illness of his grandmother who was "earnestly longing for me." From about that time on, his depression lessened, when it might have been expected to increase because he then had definite news of his grandmother's illness. He found out later, however, that at about the time he received the telegram and began to feel better, his grandmother's condition improved, the danger to her life passed, and "her yearning for my presence had decreased" (18, Vol. 1, p. 274; case 39 of Tabulation).

Case 32

Mrs. Joicey Acker Hurth, several of whose impressions I have already included (Cases 11, 12, and 29), told me during our interview in Cedarburg, Wisconsin, of another experience that occurred in 1968. Unfortunately, this one could not be corroborated because Mrs. Hurth did not tell her husband about the impression at the time. In it, she became aware that her daughter, Joicey L. Hurth, then eighteen years old, had had an accident. Mrs. Hurth's account is best given in the following portion of the transcript of our interview, at which her husband, Mr. Robert Hurth, was also present.

J.A.H.: I was sitting right there in that yellow chair and I was terrifically engrossed in it [a television program] and I suppose it must have been about middle of the way through and all of a sudden I got nervous. And I got up and began pacing around and looking out the window and thinking about Joicey. And I maybe asked Bob [Mr. Hurth] a few questions: "When did she say she would be back?" and a few things like that. And then I couldn't watch my fascinating program, and I got more and more nervous, and then I didn't want to disturb him. I just left him and went into the kitchen and I paced around and all I could think of was "ditch, ditch, ditch." The word just went through my mind over and over and over. And I thought, "Oh, Joicey is in some kind of trouble and I don't know what. But I don't think it is too terrible." And she had gone to a library in Port Washington and I knew she would be back . . . well, the library closes at 9:00 P.M.

I.S.: That's a neighboring town, is it?

J.A.H.: Yes.

R.H.: But she came home the round-about way.

J.A.H.: Yes, she did not come home the direct way, which would be a main highway. She took the long way around. And she got to a curve . . . this all came out later . . . she didn't come until midnight, and she walked in the door and I took one look at her and said, "What happened?" And she said, "I took a curve and it was just as slick as glass and my car slid right off into the ditch." And there she sat. She was with another girl and nobody came by. So she turned her lights on and just sat there waiting for somebody to come. And she said while she sat there she wondered if I wouldn't be getting nervous and worried about her coming in late. And she was thinking, "I'm all right, Mother." She told me this later. She said, "I kept thinking, I'm all right, Mother. I'm in a ditch, but I'm all right." So when she came in she told me exactly what had happened, but I had known it—that she was in some sort of trouble, I didn't know what.

I.S.: And you got the word "ditch?"

J.A.H.: I got the word "ditch" very definitely. That just went through my mind over and over. But I wasn't really terrifically upset; I knew something had happened, but I had the feeling that it wasn't that grave. I really did.

I.S.: How long did she spend in the ditch altogether?

J.A.H.: Well, she got home at midnight. The library closes at 9:00 P.M., so I presume she stayed there until it closed. She was doing a lot of research work. From about 9:30 until about, I would guess, 11:00 . . . then when somebody did find her, they had to go get a wrecker to pull her out, and all that took time. And that's the reason she didn't get home until midnight.

I.S.: And about what time did you have your experience?

J.A.H.: That show would have been at 8:00 and . . . ends at 10:00. So it was somewhere in the middle of that show.

I.S.: And when did you expect her back that night?

J.A.H.: Oh, I always . . . about 10:00 possibly. I mean, if the library closes at 9:00 and it would take her a while to get home. She might stop for a coke. I wouldn't have been upset if she had come in at 10:00 or 10:30.

I.S.: In other words, you were concerned before she was overdue?

J.A.H.: Possibly, yes. I hadn't even thought of that, but I just know that at that particular time I started getting very nervous. I had that uneasy feeling.

I.S.: But you wouldn't ordinarily have been uneasy about her being late unless it had been after 10:30, say?

J.A.H.: I possibly wouldn't have been until maybe a little later than that because sometimes they stop for a coke and it doesn't mean anything.

I.S.: Mr. Hurth, do you remember her saying anything about Joicey that night?

R.H.: No, I don't.

J.A.H.: I tried not to disturb him. He was so engrossed in . . .

R.H.: I was engrossed in TV.

J.A.H.: He doesn't like to be disturbed and so I just kept it to myself that night. I don't think I bothered him at all. I may have mentioned it, I don't know. But I have a lot of little things like that, which are almost too minute to mention—litttle things that do happen, that do come true.

Joicey L. Hurth confirmed the related event and the fact that she tried to send a mental message to her mother in a letter dated June 26, 1969, from which I quote the following:

> I cannot remember the exact date of the experience, but I do recall that it was a Wednesday evening in February, 1968. I had driven to the Port Washington Library that evening and decided to take a country route home. The road was very clear except that a right angle curve was covered with ice. The car swerved first to the right. I managed to avoid the thick trees on that side only by turning left. The car fishtailed and dove over a four-foot ditch to settle between a sign and a tree on the left side of the road, luckily in the only clear area along that stretch of road. As I could not drive back up the steep ditch, I knew I could only wait until someone came along to help.
>
> By this time it was almost 10 P.M., the hour I was expected in on school nights. I knew that Mother would soon worry, but the area was quite deserted and there was not a phone in miles.
>
> I sat back, closed my eyes and concentrated on sending

Mother a message. I mentally repeated, "I'm in a ditch, but I'm all right—don't worry."

After somewhat of a wait, I did get a ride to Cedarburg where I roused the owner of a service station who towed the car out and fixed the flat tire. I arrived home around twelve o'clock [midnight] and had not had a chance to call home. Mother was waiting up and seemed anxious, but not terribly disturbed. This was unusual because I was two hours late and hadn't called. I always try to let Mother know if I'm going to be late because I know she worries. Ordinarily, she gets extremely nervous and unable to sit still, and literally paces the floor if I am even an hour late. That night, however, she met me at the door when I came in and calmly asked, "What happened? Are you all right?"

I cannot remember the exact conversation, but I apologized for being late. She asked if I had had an accident. After I related the incident she told me that she had continuously thought the word, "ditch," from about ten o'clock on, but for some reason had felt that I was all right. I then told her about the "message" that I had tried to send her.

Subsequently, in reply to a further question from me, Joicey sent me a short statement saying that "the occasion in February, 1968, was the only time I have ever driven off the road." If Joicey had been a poor driver or liable to accidents, her mother might have had normal grounds for concern whenever her daughter was on the road in a car, but this was not the case. And Mrs. Hurth's impression had begun before Joicey was overdue at home, so this was not the explanation of her concern; nor would it alone anyway have accounted for her awareness that Joicey was in a ditch.

The foregoing case again illustrates, it would seem, the effectiveness, at least on some occasions, of the agent focusing on the percipient and directing a message to him. The message, however, does not need to be one of reassurance as to the well-being of the agent; it may be one of help or healing to the percipient, as in the case of Mme Guyon (19). Among cases of this latter type, one of the best reported is that published by Dale (6). It will be seen that in this case a two-way communication seemed to occur with a mother and her child both acting as agents and percipients:

A woman one afternoon experienced a strong awareness that her six-year-old son was drifting out to sea in a tiny boat. (All she knew normally at the time of her experience was that he had been playing with his sisters six miles away from home at a beach on Long Island Sound.) The percipient heard her boy calling "Mommie, Mommie!" She became very upset, but as she had no car she could not go to the beach. She knelt down and prayed very earnestly that her boy would be helped; that he would stay sitting in the boat, and not stand up. "I knew," she wrote, "that if he stood up, he would be lost." Before the percipient was able to verify her experience she told it to some friends, one of whom corroborated that she had done so. Later that day she learned that at the time of her experience her son was in fact drifting out to sea in a boat, but was rescued by persons who heard him calling "Mommie, Mommie!" They attributed his not being drowned to the fact that he had remained sitting in the boat instead of standing up (6, pp. 32-34).

Here then is an example in which a mother's intense love, expressed in the form of a prayer for her son's survival, and combined with a specific instruction to him, seems to have had a definite effect.

The foregoing case was not an impression experience since it included visual and auditory components. The percipients in some impression cases are, however, sometimes moved by their experience to pray for the agent. Four examples of this are included in the cases analyzed in Chapter II and listed in the Tabulation.

My own collection of materials on this subject is exceedingly scanty, but I shall describe briefly one instance of this class that was told to me by a reliable informant who was the agent in the case. Since I have no statement or corroboration from the percipient, I shall not give it a case number.

The agent's sister was undergoing a series of distressing events in her life which made her feel considerably depressed. Unknown to her sister, my informant (in another city) began to concentrate on her sister's well-being. During this time her sister began to feel better and at the same time she told their mother, with whom she was then living, that she thought my informant was trying to help her.

My informant learned of her sister's remark from her mother, who is now deceased. Since the agent of this experience is known among her family and friends for trying to help them, it would not perhaps be surprising for one of them to say that she was doing so. The importance of the incident comes then chiefly from the report of rather sudden relief experienced by the agent's sister, who at that time had no knowledge that the agent was particularly concentrating on helping her at a distance.

Cases of the type I have cited in this section may well be more numerous than the small number known to me would suggest. Their occurrence, however, underlines the need for collecting and studying additional examples if they can be found. Their importance can hardly be exaggerated for they provide some empirical evidence for the efficacy of prayer and other thoughts of good will in improving our conditions.

EXPERIENCES WITHOUT IDENTIFICATION OF AGENT

Among the 160 cases analyzed in Chapter II there were 56 (35 per cent) in which the percipient did not specifically identify the agent. In more than half of these the percipient did identify "home" or some other site as the place of trouble to which he related his impression. But in many others (nearly 17 per cent of the total number of cases) the impression consisted entirely of an unexpected, and usually sudden altered feeling state without any cognitive content whatever.

In some of these instances also the percipient did not know to what he should attribute the change in his feelings at the time. A paranormal process involved in the suddenly altered feeling state was only considered later on, when the percipient discovered a close temporal coincidence between his changed feelings and a related event, e.g., the death of the presumptive agent. Obviously, in such cases there is plenty of room for error in mistakenly attributing to a paranormal stimulus a change of feelings which may in fact have had its origin in some other unnoticed but normal stimulus. But there can be error also in failing to consider a paranormal process when feelings suddenly change without any obvious explanation.

I have already given one example (pp. 131-132) of a sudden change in a patient's feelings that may have been stimulated by extrasensory perception, and I shall now briefly recount another to emphasize my point that many experiences about which we cannot draw firm conclusions may nevertheless be instances of extrasensory perception.

Case 33

In this case the percipient, Robert Omstead (pseudonym), was, at the time of my interview with him, a psychiatric patient in the University of Virginia Hospital. He was, however, quite rational at the time of the interview and I have no reason to question the accuracy of his narration of the case, although his experience and the related death of his mother are both uncorroborated. The following information and quotations are taken from an interview I recorded with him on April 26, 1969.

Mr. Omstead's experience occurred in 1956 at the time his mother died. He had seen her twenty-seven days before her death and she seemed to be in excellent health. Nevertheless, she died suddenly of heart disease at about 5:30 A.M. on October 1, 1956. At the time the percipient was living in Elizabethtown, Kentucky, and his mother was living in West Point, Virginia, seven hundred miles away.

On the morning of his mother's death Mr. Omstead awoke early at 5:30 A.M. He said he was startled. "I felt that somebody had shook me awake. . . . I felt this dread feeling, this real dread feeling." He could not get back to sleep. When his wife, who woke up later, asked him what the trouble was, he told her: "I have the strangest feeling that something is wrong. I can't put my hands on it, but I have a very empty feeling. I felt that before, but it didn't work out like this did. [Here the informant is evidently referring to another occasion when he had a similar feeling that was not identified by him as related to a specific event.] So I was telling her [his wife] at breakfast and I emphasized the fact that I felt real empty and I knew something was wrong."

Mr. Omstead was ordinarily a heavy sleeper, difficult to arouse in the morning. His usual waking time in the morning was 6:00 A.M. He recalled having awakened as early as on this occasion only once before in his life.

At about 7:00 A.M. Mr. Omstead proceeded to the military camp where he worked and there at about 8:00 A.M. received a telephone call from his wife. It was unusual for her to call him so soon after he had left the house and therefore natural for him to surmise that she would only have done so for bad news. When he answered the telephone his wife said she had some bad news to tell him and he replied: "Is it mother?" His wife replied that it was and he then said: "She's dead." His mother had died in her bed at about 5:30 A.M. His father had discovered her in a terminal convulsion and she died soon after. His father had telephoned his son's wife, who then reached him at his work. His mother's death had been quite unexpected. The percipient immediately related the news to what he had felt earlier in the morning. He said: ". . . that was the answer to my feeling, that empty feeling."

We may not join the percipient in his conclusion with so much firmness for he did not relate his feeling of "emptiness" and dread when he awakened to his mother or to anyone else. He merely felt that "something is wrong." And his later connection of the feeling to his mother only occurred when he heard from his wife over the telephone that she had bad news to relate. Nevertheless, we have Mr. Omstead's word that he only once before in his life woke early with a similar feeling, and it may well be that his abnormally early awakening and feeling of malaise on this occasion are best interpreted as stimulated by an extrasensory communication related to his mother's almost simultaneous death. If Mr. Omstead had thought of his mother in connection with his feeling of emptiness and dread, we would more confidently assign a paranormal element to his experience. But merely because he did not identify the (possible) agent does not mean there was no extrasensory perception in the case. It may be another example of a paranormal impression without identification of the agent and a further reminder of the possibility that unusual changes of feelings may arise through extrasensory perception much more often than most persons realize.

Experiences Involving More than One Percipient

What we might call collective impression experiences are rare, but a few have occurred and been reported. The cases analyzed in Chapter II of this monograph include three examples.

In the first of these, a woman had an impression during the night that her mother was seriously ill. Despite her husband's protests she went to see her mother and as she approached her mother's house she met her sister, who had had a similar impression and had also acted on her impulse to see their mother. The sisters found that in fact their mother had been taken suddenly ill, was dying, and had asked to see her daughters (Case 36 of Tabulation).

In the second case, a man and a young boy became simultaneously but independently aware that the boy's mother needed him. The boy went to his mother and found that she did need him very much at this time because of an uncle's sudden illness (Case 91 of Tabulation).

In the third case, a whole family seems to have been affected. The members of this farm family, eight in number, arose one morning, had their breakfasts, and then dispersed to various points for the day's work. Later in the morning the family members each stopped work and returned to the kitchen. "About ten o'clock a strange feeling possessed the whole family, young and old alike. Each thought it some coming illness though they felt no pain, simply an intense awe, a dread foreboding as if something awful was about to happen. Everyone thought it peculiar to himself and only learned that others of the family were affected the same way when they reached the kitchen." This quite unusual behavior of the family coincided in time with the accidental death of a son of the family who was killed in Michigan. The affected family lived in northern New York (26, pp. 149-153; case 101 of Tabulation).

From the account of this case it seems possible, if not probable,

that some of the members of the family who were working together may have affected each other's behavior normally. But
other individuals or pairs were separated and they seem to have
responded independently to the communication.

Matthews reported a case of collective percipience occurring
among separated persons. The subjects were natives of the Bahamas, members of a religious sect, who participated in communal
ecstasies and "fits." The tendency to such "fits" spread. To quote
Matthews:

> These attacks spread like wildfire through the whole island.
> Villages at distances of 10, 15, and 30 miles from each other
> were affected simultaneously, though it is almost certain they
> had no communication with each other. Girls at work in fields
> would be seized suddenly, and had to be carried home. . . .
>
> I have sat in a house in attendance upon a patient [a mem-
> ber of this sect] when suddenly she would begin to twitch and
> shake, and finally succumb to a fit. I found out that the precise
> moment she was seized, other girls in the meeting had been
> taken too. This was a remarkable thing and scared the people
> considerably (31, p. 486).

The idea of group percipience of feelings is well developed,
although I know not on what evidence, among shamans and
modern spiritualists. Both these groups hold that for the successful development of "power" an appropriate feeling must be
generated in the attending persons. They may well be right and
the possibility certainly deserves investigation.

It is further possible that paranormal processes affecting groups
may contribute to the greater than ordinary tendencies toward
irrational behavior in mobs or toward courageous actions of groups
such as soldiers fighting a battle together. Hitherto these group
excesses beyond what might be expected of individuals acting
alone have seemed sufficiently explained by the power of suggestion and the tendencies of persons to submit themselves to
leadership acting through entirely normal means of communication.
But it is at least possible that some of the effects observed in
group behavior may arise from the reverberation of feelings and
intentions shared through extrasensory processes.

Chapter Five

THE PROCESSES OF COMMUNICATION

Introductory Remarks

Impression experiences suggest several questions and some tentative answers about the processes involved in extrasensory communication. I shall first consider why some persons (at some times) have impression experiences instead of imaged ones.

The "standard" fully developed impression experience consists of (a) a cognitive awareness that a particular person is in distress and needs help; (b) a feeling or emotion appropriate to that awareness, and (c) an impulse toward action to help the distressed person. In even more fully developed experiences additional details, e.g., that the agent is dying, or visual or auditory imagery become added, and the agent or his surroundings may be briefly seen or heard.

At the other end of the scale of development, however, we find *formes frustes* of the impression experience in which only a portion of the potential experience manifests. Thus we have cases with the following characteristics:

1. Impaired cognitive awareness so that there is localization of the site of the trouble, e.g., "home," but no penetration into consciousness of the person involved in the trouble, e.g., the percipient's child. These cases remind one of the partial remembrance of a name one has forgotten in which one recalls the initial or the first syllable of the name, but cannot get the whole word out of the memory bank (79).

2. Cases even more stunted than the foregoing, in which there is no cognitive aspect whatever, but only either:

(a) Pure feeling or emotion in which the percipient experiences an unusual, or at least unexpected, emotion appropriate to the (unconscious) knowledge of the distress of the agent whom, however, the percipient does not identify; or

(b) Pure motor impulse in which the percipient experiences no cognitive information and no emotion, but has an impulse to go toward the site of presumable trouble. He acts like a puppet or a person under the influence of a posthypnotic suggestion. (The experience of Mrs. O'Brien (Case 10) may be regarded as providing an example of almost pure motor response, and Nicol and Nicol (38; case 122 of Tabulation) published a well-authenticated example of this type); or

(c) Pain or other physical symptoms in the percipient either imitating similar symptoms in the agent or precipitated by (unconscious) knowledge of the agent's distress.

. There are differences also along another axis between the experience of the agent and that of the percipient. As we have seen, some percipients experience an emotion, e.g., anxiety, or a physical symptom, e.g., pain, which resembles or, as it were, copies the same condition in the agent. The percipients who have uterine hemorrhages or uterine pains when their daughters go into labor provide examples of this type of response. Other percipients, however, under the stimulus of the communication from the agent, initiate a response of their own, reacting to, but not imitating, the condition of the agent. Thus we have percipients who are depressed and grieving over the death of the agent. And one percipient experienced joy in relation to her apparently paranormal awareness of her sister's death (Case 105 of Tabulation). We also have percipients who may develop a physical illness, e.g., asthma, in response to a telepathically communicated stress in a loved agent, but the agent does not have asthma which is, however, a characteristic mode of the percipient's responses to stress.

Why extrasensory communications find their way into conscious and manifest expression in these different ways in different people we do not yet understand. The analysis of a large number of cases might well show that imagery, for example, develops more readily in percipients who are good visual imagers in other aspects of life and that perhaps physical symptoms develop more readily in persons liable to react with physical symptoms to other types of stress. And, as I have suggested earlier, the imitative type of expression of a telepathic communication may occur more frequently in those given otherwise to strong identifications with other persons. These are questions of great importance. Their solution will require the investigation of large numbers of cases and the alliance in one person, or in several, of the skills of the student of spontaneous cases, of the clinical psychologist, and perhaps of the experimental parapsychologist.

The reports of percipients suggest that they usually receive into consciousness first a general impression that something is wrong, and then specific details regarding, for example, who is in trouble and how. Note Mrs. Hurth's depression with weeping and awareness that something was wrong, and then—at breakfast— her localization of her distress to an awareness that something was wrong with her father (Case 11). Sometimes the percipient cannot make any better localization of the source of the impression. Mrs. Hellström, for example, said that in one of her impression experiences (Case 20) she definitely did *not* know that her husband was ill. All she knew was that she felt uneasy and that she must go home. Nor did her impressions of her friend Jan convey *what* was troubling him, only that he was (usually) in distress. She merely had a strong feeling of depression or fatigue which she somehow connected with him. Yet in other cases, the percipient does somehow get additional details into consciousness.

Mrs. Rudkin (Case 1), for example, not only identified her mother, but to the astonishment of her family flatly asserted that she had died. So did Mrs. Jensen (Case 9). And Mrs. Sternberg (Case 3) knew not only that her son was ill, but also that he was in the hospital. Similarly, Mrs. Heywood once had an impression experience that included fairly detailed instructions about getting to a railway station earlier than expected to meet her husband and arrange to have a porter on hand (21, pp. 47-48). And in a case reported by Dale *et al.*, the percipient became aware that her mother needed money and further, that the sum needed seemed like either $15 or $10. She sent her mother $10 and her letter enclosing this crossed in the mails with one from her mother asking her daughter to send her $10. She had never before asked for money or seemed to need it. She had actually needed $15, but decided to ask for only $10 (7, pp. 32-34; case 123 of Tabulation). Cases with such additional details suggest that at some level the percipient may actually receive a more complete communication, but that only part of it manages to emerge into consciousness.

There is an interesting similarity here between impression cases which have little detail and certain dreams and imaged extrasensory experiences. Many dreamers experience "presences" in the dreams which they cannot see, but remain aware of. The unseen person is in the dream and playing an active part, but is invisible. The dreamer will say afterwards, for example, "Then I was back home and I felt somehow that my Aunt Susan was in the room, but I could not see her. She just seemed to be there."

The partial and sometimes distorted or misinterpreted emergence into consciousness of what may, for convenience, be called "telepathic signals" is illustrated by the successful attempts of Mrs. Craig Sinclair to perceive target drawings which were experimentally "transmitted" by other persons (63). Her remarkable "hits" in these experiments have been acknowledged by such expert investigators as W. F. Prince (45) and E. M. Sidgwick (62), but in the study of process Mrs. Sinclair's "half hits" may be even more instructive. Sometimes she would get the general "field" of the target drawing, but not the drawing itself. When, for instance, the target was a glass of water, she said, "Think of a saucer, then of a cup. It's something in the kitchen." On another occasion she said:

> I once saw a circle and *felt* that it was an automobile wheel —felt it so vividly that I became overwhelmed with curiosity to see if my "feeling" was correct, and forthwith turned on the light and examined the real picture. . . . I found that it was indeed the wheel of an automobile. But I do not do this kind of thing unless I have a very decided "hunch" as it tends to lead back to the natural impulse of the mind to "guess"—and

guessing is one of the things one has to strive to avoid. To a
certain extent, one comes to know the difference between a guess
and a "hunch" (63, p. 117).

Gilbert Murray, who was the percipient in a remarkable
series of experiments, was also a sensitive observer of the development of his correct knowledge of the target at which he was
aiming. In discussing hypotheses such as hyperesthesia as alter-
natives to the explanation of telepathy for his experiences, Murray
said:

> Of course, the personal impression of the percipient himself
> is by no means conclusive evidence, but I do feel there is one
> almost universal quality in these guesses of mine which does suit
> telepathy and does not suit any other explanation. They always
> begin with a vague emotional quality of atmosphere: "This is
> horrible, this is grotesque, this is full of anxiety"; or rarely, "This
> is something delightful"; or sometimes, "This is out of a book,"
> "This is a Russian novel," or the like. That seems like a direct
> impression of some human mind. Even in the failures this feeling
> of atmosphere often gets through. That is, it was not so much
> an act of cognition, or a piece of information that was transferred
> to me, but rather a feeling or an emotion; and it is notable that
> I never had any success on guessing mere cards or numbers, or
> any subject that was not in some way interesting or amusing
> (33, p. 163).

A few examples from Murray's telepathic experiences will
illustrate his point:

> When the subject was "Bavarian peasants in a dancing-room
> drinking beer by a wooden table in a room full of smoke,"
> Murray said: "People dancing—in a funny costume, I think—
> not court dress—rather ugly, rather lumpy peasant costume . . ."
> (76, p. 92).
> When the subject was "Little Mermaid in Andersen's Fairy-
> tales at the bottom of the sea," Murray said: "Poem or picture
> to do with the sea—it seems like a mermaid sitting on a rock"
> 76, p. 93).

When the subject was "Celia Newbolt under a gourd tree at Smyrna," Murray said: "Modern Greek of some kind—sort of Asia Minor place—a tree and women sitting under it—a particular tree—a girl sitting under it—she does not belong to the place—she is English . . ." (76, pp. 107-108).

These examples and some of the impression cases closely resemble the process (studied by Wenzl) of remembering a name one has temporarily forgotten, but "really knows." A part of the name may emerge into consciousness, usually the first letter or syllable, and also perhaps its length or associations. Say it were Jensen, then the letter "J" might be recalled and that the name was Scandinavian. But that might be all (79).

We have known since the end of the last century that in extrasensory communication the transmission (if I may use this term without commitment to a particular theory) from one person to another occurs unconsciously. This phase of the total process may be, for all we know, quite perfect at the level of reception in unconscious strata of the percipient's mind. The second stage of the process occurs solely within the percipient's mind as the communication is mediated into consciousness and/or into emotions and actions (74).

We need to ask then what prevents the communication of impressions from developing into fully detailed information. This is a large question and speculation about it can only be very tentative. But four possible interfering factors suggest themselves.

1. Part of the percipient's mind may not want to know the whole story. Nobody welcomes bad news and a process of selective inattention may block its full emergence (39). La Rochefoucauld's aphorism that "we all have strength to bear our friends' misfortunes" includes the corollary that we may prefer not even to hear of them. Fortunately this is not always so, for the condition of love notably includes a willingness to share another's burdens. Still, it may be that in some cases the ambivalent attitude of a percipient toward a particular agent may explain the lack of detail and imagery in his impressions. But ambivalent attitudes certainly did not dominate the powerful urges of some of the

percipients of the present cases to help the apparent agents of their impressions.

2. A second image-inhibiting factor may be the percipient's strong emotional reaction to a "telepathic signal" which blocks out detailed perceptions. Both everyday clinical observations and experimental work have shown that strong emotions, especially anxiety, restrict the field of attention and diminish peripheral perceptions (4); and it is clear from their descriptions that many of the percipients of these impression cases became fully "taken over," as it were, by the emotional quality of their experiences. As already mentioned, 52 per cent of the percipients whose cases I analyzed in Chapter II took action based on their impressions. (More than 50 per cent of the percipients in the newly reported cases of this monograph took action; see summary analysis in Chapter VI to follow.) As my examples have abundantly illustrated, the pressure toward action on the part of the percipient was often very strong, and indeed often led to behavior which seemed quite irrational to other persons. The percipients often behaved, in fact, like persons who have only one thing on their minds and pay no attention to anything else. This condition is the opposite of the relaxed expectancy which White, after studying a large number of successful percipients, has described as favoring imaged extra-sensory perception (82). Thus, once the percipient has been "taken over" by his conviction that something is wrong which he must try to remedy, his conscious mind may be less "permeable" to imagery which could have reached it in a more tranquil state.

The feeling of conviction occurs much more often in impression cases than in dreams or waking hallucinations. For example, in L. E. Rhine's series, 84 per cent of the impression (called by her intuitive) experiences included a sense of conviction (defined as the percipient's taking action or making a clear statement about conviction) as opposed to only 21 per cent of the (realistic) dream cases (49). In the (1960) S.P.R. survey of spontaneous cases the feeling of conviction occurred in 37 per cent of the impression cases, in 14 per cent of the dreams, and in only 9 per cent of the waking hallucinations (17, p. 135). These marked discrepancies invite a much fuller analysis of patterns, and especially of personality patterns in the different types of cases.

Are, for example, persons who have impression type experiences more likely to be otherwise somewhat impulsive and given to action rather than to introspection? Certainly not always, we can answer, since some percipients, e.g., Mrs. Hellström, have *both* impression experiences and imaged ones on different occasions. Mrs. Hellström recorded twelve impression experiences in her diary, but many more imaged experiences. Mrs. Hurth (Cases 11, 12, 29, and 32), Mr. Judd (Case 13), Mr. Melrose (Case 15), Mrs. Schlotterbeck (Case 28), and Mrs. Bolles (Case 31) have all had both impression and imaged experiences. And Mrs. Heywood, another critical observer of her own experiences, has had both impression experiences (Cases 22 and 23) and, at other times, experiences with imagery (21). Shifting attitudes or other conditions in a percipient may account for the variations in the form of his extrasensory experiences at different times. It is also probable that different persons have different capacities for bringing unconscious mental contents into consciousness in the form of images. We know that persons differ considerably in their capacity for imaged memories and eidetic imagery, and it seems likely that such differences in imaging capacity also have an important influence on the form of extrasensory perceptions.

3. Action taken by the percipient in response to his impression is negatively correlated with the emergence of additional details. This suggests that the physical activity involved in the action may inhibit emergence of more detail in the communication, although it is possible that we are here dealing again with an inhibiting effect of emotion, since strong emotion seems usually to have accompanied the taking of action by the percipients.

4. The percipient's circumstances may not favor the full development of imagery. Situations which reduce sensory stimuli, e.g., sleeping, are more often associated with imaged extrasensory perceptions and the waking state more often associated with impression experiences. L. E. Rhine found that in 308 impression (intuitive) cases, *all* occurred during the waking state (47). Table 6 shows that only 17 (approximately 10 per cent) of the percipients in the 160 cases analyzed in Chapter II were asleep when they first had their impressions.

In 71 of the 125 occasions for which we have information, the percipient was with other people at the time of having the impression; in the remaining 54 occasions he was alone (Table 6). The question then arises whether a subject who was with other people would have perceived more details of the presumed message if he had been alone. As indicated in Column 9 of the Tabulation, 58 percipients did perceive more details, including such items as that the agent had died, or been hit on the head, or been admitted to a hospital and so on. In 47 of these 58 cases we have information on whether the percipient was alone or with other people at the time of the impression. In 24 cases the percipient was alone and in 23 he was with others, not a significant difference. So far as these data go, then, it would seem that merely being with other persons does not block the communication of additional details. But, as I have already said, a person in company may still be lost in reverie and inwardly open to the upwelling of detailed communications. Nevertheless, the full withdrawal of attention from external stimuli (as in sleep or profound concentration) cannot occur often in the presence of other persons, least of all on ordinary social occasions, so it seems likely that other persons do usually have some inhibiting effect. If this be so, many reported impressions might have included sensory imagery had the communication occurred during sleep or if the percipient could have developed the imagery in seclusion.

To illustrate the influence of the presence of other persons on the total experience, I shall first cite a rather uncomplicated case from *Phantasms of the Living:*

> All at once a dreadful feeling of illness and faintness came over me, and I felt that I was dying. I had no power to get up to ring the bell for assistance, but sat with my head in my hands utterly helpless.
>
> My maid came into the room for the tea things. I thought I would keep her with me, but felt better while she was there, so did not mention my illness to her, thinking it had passed away. However, as soon as I lost the sound of her footsteps, it all came back upon me worse than ever . . . (18, Vol. 1, p. 273; case 2 of Tabulation).

The above impression coincided closely in time with the sudden onset of an unexpected illness in the percipient's husband, who was then at his office.

Persons undergoing some strong negative emotion very commonly, almost usually, move toward other persons for comfort and reassurance. Several of the percipients of the cases analyzed in Chapter II did this. However, when, as in these cases and the one just cited, the general distress of the percipient diminishes while he is with other persons, we cannot decide whether the presence of others has reduced the percipient's distress directly by reassuring companionship or indirectly by distracting him and thus interfering with the emergence of the extrasensory communication into consciousness.

The analysis in Chapter II brought out some other factors (additional to the four just discussed) relevant to the emergence of detail in impression cases. It was found in that analysis that agent focusing on the percipient was not correlated with the occurrence of additional details; nor was the gravity of the agent's situation, e.g., whether or not he was dying. On the other hand, agent focusing was significantly correlated with action on the part of the percipient.

THE DEVELOPMENT OF ADDITIONAL DETAILS OR OF IMAGERY AFTER AN INITIAL IMPRESSION

It sometimes happens that the percipient can successfully bring additional details or actual imagery to the surface of consciousness after he has had an initial general impression. I think this process so important that I propose to quote several published cases at length and to present one that I investigated myself.

The first example comes from one of the cases analyzed in Chapter II. The percipient's account clearly described the development of the impression in stages of increasing clarity as to the agent's wish. The percipient stated:

> My mother had gone out [of the house] with the rest to the tennis ground. [The percipient remained in the house.] Feeling it cold, she sent my youngest brother, H., for her white shawl. I

met him halfway between the tennis ground and the house carrying the aforesaid shawl [myself]. The reasons for this were[1]:

(a) At the time that my mother asked my brother to get her the shawl, I felt an impression that I must do something.

(b) This gradually increased in intensity till I knew that my mother wanted a shawl;

(c) then, as if by another stage of completer intuition, I knew it was a white shawl,

(d) and I knew that I had to go to the drawing-room to fetch it (though I did not previously know it was there). So I went and fetched it and brought it to my mother, as I felt obliged to (46, p. 172; case 71 of Tabulation).

The percipient in the second example, published in *Human Personality,* said that he had himself been a "witness" of psychical phenomena for many years, but had never before had a personal experience of this type. He seems to have possessed unusually steady nerves for he held himself attentive for some minutes while an invisible "presence" developed into the veridical image of a friend who had just had a serious accident:

On the evening of February 10th, 1894, I was sitting in my room expecting the return of two friends from a concert in the provinces where they had been performing. The friends in question had lived with me for some years, and we were more than usually attached to one another. . . .

On the day mentioned they were performing at an afternoon concert, and I had every reason to believe they would be tired and get home as soon as possible. I allowed half-an-hour beyond the usual time (10:30 P.M.) of arrival to elapse before I got at all uneasy, speculating as people will under such circumstances as to what was keeping them, although arguing to myself all the time that there was not the slightest occasion for alarm. I then took up a book in which I was much in-

---

[1] I have set off the different stages in separate paragraphs for emphasis. In the original report these sentences were in one paragraph.

terested, sitting in an easy chair before the fire with a reading-lamp close to my right side, and in such a position that only by deliberately turning round could I see the window on my left, before which heavy chenille curtains were drawn. I had read some twenty minutes or so, was thoroughly absorbed in the book, my mind was perfectly quiet, and for the time being my friends were quite forgotten, when suddenly without a moment's warning my whole being seemed roused to the highest state of tension or aliveness, and I was aware, with an intenseness not easily imagined by those who have never experienced it, that another being or presence was not only in the room but close to me. I put my book down, and although my excitement was great, I felt quite collected and not conscious of any sense of fear. Without changing my position, and looking straight at the fire, I knew somehow that my friend A. H. was standing at my left elbow, but so far behind me as to be hidden by the arm-chair in which I was leaning back. Moving my eyes round slightly without otherwise changing my position, the lower portion of one leg became visible, and I instantly recognised the grey-blue material of trousers he often wore, but the stuff appeared semi-transparent, reminding me of tobacco smoke in consistency. I could have touched it with my hand without moving more than my left arm. With that curious instinctive wish not to see more of such a "figure," I did no more than glance once or twice at the apparition and then directed my gaze steadily at the fire in front of me. An appreciable space of time passed—probably several seconds in all, but seeming in reality much longer—when the most curious thing happened. Standing upright between me and the window on my left, and at a distance of about four feet from me and almost immediately behind my chair, I saw perfectly the figure of my friend—the face very pale, the head slightly thrown back, the eyes shut, and on one side of the throat, just under the jaw, a wound with blood on it. The figure remained motionless with the arms close to the sides, and for some time, how long I can't say, I looked steadily at it; then all at once roused myself, turned deliberately round, the figure vanished, and I realised instantly that I had seen the figure behind me without moving from my first position—an impossible feat physically. I am perfectly certain I never moved my position from the first appearance of the figure as seen physically, until it disappeared on my turning round (37, Vol. 1, pp. 672-673).

Myers interviewed both the percipient and a witness to the accident and was satisfied that A.H.'s accident occurred approximately simultaneously with the appearance of the apparition. A.H. had fallen and struck his jaw against the curb. When he was brought home, his jaw was still bleeding and his face was pale from shock.

This case, incidentally, permits one possible answer to the question "Why do apparitions vanish?" It seems clear that awareness of them (when the experience contains veridical elements) implies some extrasensory process, even were we to grant them some kind of substantial form. Such a form might move out of the percipient's field of vision, if a limitation of "fields" exists for extrasensory perception. But an apparition could also vanish, not because it moved away, but because the mental state of the percipient altered. The percipient in the case just cited stated that it was when he roused himself and deliberately turned around that the figure vanished, and these actions would presumably induce changes in him which would be the opposite of those which, a few minutes earlier, had enabled him to develop the invisible "presence" into a full sensory image.

Another case was reported in *Human Personality* in which an impression also developed into an imaged perception. The percipient described it in a letter of October 16, 1883:

My wife went to reside at the seaside on September 30th last, taking with her our youngest child, a little boy thirteen months old.

On Wednesday, October 3rd, I felt a strong impression that the little fellow was worse (he was in weak health on his departure). The idea then prevailed on my mind that he had met with a slight accident; and immediately the picture of the bedroom in which he sleeps appeared in my mind's eye. It was *not* the strong sensation of awe or sorrow, as I had often experienced before on such occasions; but, anyhow, I fancied he had fallen *out of the bed,* upon chairs, and then rolled down upon the floor. This was about 11 A.M., and I at once wrote to my wife, asking her to let me know how the little fellow was getting on. I thought it rather bold to tell my wife that the baby had, to my conviction, really met with an accident, without being able to produce any confirmatory evidence. Also I considered that she would take it as an insinuation of carelessness on her part; therefore I purposely wrote it as a *post scriptum*.

I heard no more about it, and even fancied that this time my impression was merely the consequence of anxiety. But on Saturday last I went to see my wife and child, and asked whether she had taken notice of my advice to protect the baby against such an accident. She smiled at first, and then informed me that he had tumbled out of the bed upon the chairs placed at the side, and then found his way upon the floor, without being hurt. She further remarked, "You must have been thinking of that when it was just too late, because it happened the same day your letter came, some hours previously." I asked her what time of the day it happened. Answer: "About 11 A.M." She told me that she heard the baby fall, and at once ran upstairs to pick him up.

I am certain, without the shadow of a doubt, that I wrote immediately after the impression; and that this was between 11 and 11:30 in the morning.

Gurney, who investigated the case, made the following statement:

I have seen the letter which Mr. Keulemans wrote to his wife. The envelope bears the post-mark of Worthing, October 3rd; and the postscript contained the following words: "Mind little Gaston does not fall out of bed. Put chairs in front of it. You know accidents soon happen. The fact is, I am almost certain he has met with such a mishap this very morning." (37, Vol. I, pp. 662-663).

A day or two after Mr. Keulemans reported on his experience, Mrs. Keulemans' aunt supplied the following testimony: "Mrs. Keulemans (my niece) and her baby are staying at my house. The baby had fallen out of bed the morning of the day the letter [i.e., Mr. Keulemans' letter of October 3rd to his wife] was received."

Mr. Keulemans had other experiences of a similar kind and

moreover wrote out his own account of the process, as he understood it, whereby impressions developed into imaged perceptions.
His account deserves to be quoted, together with another example
of his experiences:

My profession is that of a scientific artist. I draw a good
deal on stone; and my principal subjects are birds and animals.
It so happens that the eye of a bird, during the slow process of
drawing it, forms a capital point for concentration of the mind
and consequent distraction from ordinary flows of thought. I
noticed that whenever strong impressions had got hold of my
mind they had a tendency to develop themselves into a vivid
mind-picture as soon as my eye and attention were concentrated
upon the eye in the drawing; and that whenever I began
darkening the iris, leaving the light speck the most prominent
part, I would slowly pass off into a kind of dream-state. The
mere act of drawing the eye is not enough to bring me into
this state, or I should experience such a state at least once a
day, which I do not. But if a strong mental impression takes
hold of me I begin drawing an eye, since I know from experience that such an impression means that something has
occurred which, so to say, comes within reach of my centre of
mental attraction. The drawing will then convey to me the news,
either in the form of a vague, imperfect representation of the
person indicated in the impression, or by a correct hallucinatory
picture of the event as it actually occurred, both as regards the
person and the surroundings. Sometimes I cannot get at the
vision at once; other thoughts and scenes interfere. But when
I begin to feel drowsy I know I shall have it right in a second;
and here I lose normal consciousness. That there is an actual
loss of consciousness I know from the fact that on one occasion
my wife had been in the room talking to me, and not receiving a
reply thought that something was wrong with me and shook my
shoulder. The shake brought me back to my waking state.

Telepathic Instance. . . . Last summer, in Paris, I experienced
a picture of the vaguer class. I first had a strong notion that
something was wrong somewhere, affecting a near relative. As the
notion kept disturbing me, I resorted to my bird's eye experiment,
and saw my wife and mother-in-law moving hurriedly in my

bedroom here at Southend. I then heard my child, little Marie, scream; not a painful outcry, rather an outburst of temper. This happened at about 1 P.M. I wrote home asking for particulars and posted the letter at 4 P.M. At 9 P.M. I was with a friend at Montreuil, near Paris. The family were finishing their dinner, and I walked into the garden, when I saw hallucinatorily, without any experimental means, a picture of our bedroom, and little Marie in sound sleep. I heard my boys laugh. It was all right again at home, said the telepathic "message." Two days later my wife wrote that I had been correct in my perception of little Marie's condition. She had been very ill during the day —a kind of fit caused by the presence of thread-worms; but by nine o'clock, after vigorous treatment, was better, and went to sleep. Here the message was correct so far as the person was concerned; but there was flaw in the visualisation of the surroundings, since Marie had not been in our bedroom, but in the nursery (24, p. 517).

The next case comes from *Phantasms of the Living*. It will be noticed that the experience started with an impression while the percipient was with others; when alone shortly afterwards he developed the perception of an apparition of his brother, who, as he learned later, had died unexpectedly at that time.

Some months before his demise, my brother (Senator Carlo Fenzi) one day, as we were driving to town together from our villa of St. Andrea, told me that if he should be summoned first, he would endeavour to prove to me that life continued beyond the chasm of the grave, and that I was to promise him the same in case I went first; *"but,"* said he, "I am sure to go first, and, mind you, I feel quite sure that before the year is out—nay, in three months—I shall be no more." This was said in June and he died on the 2nd of September, the same year, 1881.

Now, on that fatal morning (the 2nd of September), I was some 70 miles away from Florence, namely, at Fortullino, a villa of ours on a rock on the sea, 10 miles south-east of Leghorn. Well, at about half-past 10 in the morning, I was seized with a fit of deep melancholy—a thing very unusual with me, who enjoy great serenity of mind. I had, however, no reason for being alarmed about my brother, who was then in Florence—as, although he had not been very well, the latest news of him was very good, as my nephew had written to say, *"Uncle is doing very comfortably, and it cannot even be said that he has really been ill"*—so that I could not account for this sudden gloomy impression; yet the tears stood in my eyes, and in order not to burst out crying like a baby before our family party, I rushed out of the house without my hat on, although it was blowing a hurricane, and the rain fell in torrents, accompanied by permanent flashes of lightning, and the loud and unceasing roar of the sea and of thunder.

I ran and ran, and only stopped when I had reached the end of a spacious lawn, from whence are seen, close on the other side of a small stream (the Fortulla), the huge stones or rocks heaped on one another, and stretching for a good half mile along the sea coast. I there gazed to try and see a youth, a cousin of mine, who, having been born among the Zulus, retained enough of love for savage life to have yielded to the wish of going out in that terrible weather, "to enjoy," he said, "the fury of the elements." Judge of my surprise and astonishment when, instead of Giovanni (such is my cousin's name), I saw my brother, with a top hat and his big white moustachios, stepping leisurely along from one rock to another, as if the weather were fair and calm! I could not believe my eyes; and yet, there he was—he, unmistakably! I thought of rushing back to the house to call every one out to give him a hearty welcome, but then preferred waiting for him, and meanwhile waved my hand to him and called out his name as loud as I possibly could, although with the awful noise of wind, and sea, and thunder combined, nothing could naturally be heard. He meanwhile continued to advance, until, having reached a rock larger than the rest, he slipped behind it. The distance between myself and the rock was, as nearly as I can judge, not more than 60 paces. I waited for him to reappear on the other side—but to no purpose, and I only saw Giovanni, who was just then emerging from a wood, and stepping on to the rocks. Giovanni, tall and slight, with a broad-brimmed hat and dark beard, was altogether a very different type, and I thought that my having seen Charles, my brother, must have been a freak of my sense of vision, and felt rather annoyed, and almost blushed at the idea that I could have been so deceived by a sort of phantom of my own fancy; yet could not help telling Giovanni, "There must be some family likeness, for I must positively have taken you for Charles, although I cannot make out how you could have gone from behind the huge rock into the wood without my seeing you cross over." *"I never was behind the rock,"* he said, *"for when you saw me, I had but just put my foot on the rocks."*

Meanwhile [I] went home, put on fresh clothes, and then joined the rest to breakfast. My melancholy had left me, and I conversed merrily with all the young people. After breakfast a telegram came, telling me and my daughter Christina to hasten home, as Carlo had suddenly been taken very ill. We made preparations to at once depart, and meanwhile another telegram came, urging us to make all possible haste, as the illness was making rapid strides, but although we caught the nearest train, we only arrived in Florence at night; where we found, to our horror, that my brother had died just at the time when in the morning I had seen him on the rocks, when, feeling that his moments were numbered, he had been continually asking for me, regretting not to see me appear.

In kissing his cold forehead with intense sorrow, as we had lived together, and loved one another during our whole lives, I thought, "Poor, dear Charlie; *he kept his word!*" (18, Vol. 2 pp. 63-65).

Case 34

The following case illustrates the development of an experience from a simple impression to an imaged form corresponding to the usual apparitional experience. It was first reported to me by the percipient, Mrs. Brigitte Judd, who is the wife of Mr. J. W. Judd, the percipient of Case 13. I quote from her letter to me dated December 11, 1967:

On a Wednesday night—Aug. 3, 1966—I had the distinct feeling that my mother-in-law wanted me to call her. In my mind I kept telling her that it was as far from her to her phone as it was for me to reach my phone and since she caused the rift [a family disagreement] she could jolly well call us. She did not let me be. The sensation persisted and grew stronger until I actually saw her, my [step] father-in-law with her, standing in front of our master-bathroom, with their hands extended as if to shake my hand. The appearance or picture was so strong that I actually stretched out my own hand, but before I touched them I told myself that this is nonsense, they are not here, you're tired, etc. My husband saw my expression and asked me about it. I told him that mother-in-law wanted me to call her and that I had just seen them. Without a further word, he jumped into his car and drove over [to his mother's house]. When he returned, he told me that their house was dark, but that [my] sister-in-law's house (she had not spoken to us for two years either) was brightly lit. This was on Friday, August 5th, 1966. On the next morning, Saturday, August 6th, my husband called me to his side and showed me a picture in the newspaper. It was a picture of my [step] father-in-law and the accompanying story told that he, my mother-in-law and the other lady [who had accompanied them] were overdue on their return from a fishing trip in Mexico. We went to see [my husband's] sister and she was quietly hysterical about her parents' unexplained absence.

Mr. J. W. Judd, the percipient's husband (who himself later had some imaged perceptions related to the same events), signed a statement testifying as follows: "The above description of events by my wife, Brigitte Judd, accords with my recollection of these same events."

In response to a question from me concerning whether Mrs. Judd had ever before had an impression that her mother-in-law wanted her to call, Mr. Judd wrote, in a letter dated February 3, 1969, as follows: "As far as I know, my wife has never had impressions that my mother was in danger, and has had no other vision of her."

Mr. and Mrs. Judd also sent me clippings from a newspaper (dated August 12, 1966) of the California town in which Mr. Judd's mother lives. The clippings narrated the harrowing ordeal which she and the other two members of her party experienced when they were lost in the Gulf of California for twelve days in 1966. The engine of their small cabin cruiser had failed and they drifted far away from settlements and assistance. They were close to death from dehydration when they were finally rescued.

In a letter to me dated January 9, 1968, Mrs. Judd said: "I wish to repeat that there had been a definite family rift two years prior to the incident and neither he [her husband] nor I had any knowledge of a planned fishing trip or any other trip by my in-laws. We had not communicated for two years."

In June 1969 I interviewed Mr. and Mrs. Judd in Upland, California, about this and other paranormal experiences they have had, e.g., Case 13. Some further details not mentioned above came out during this interview.

Mrs. Judd said that the impression that her mother-in-law wanted her had actually lasted about a week before the evening on which she had the vision. According to the newspaper reports, the victims of the near-tragedy in the Gulf of California had driven to Mexico on July 26, 1966. They did not run into trouble, however, until July 28, when the engine of their boat failed and the boat drifted onto the rocks. This was a week before Mrs. Judd's apparitional experience and so the onset of her impression that her mother-in-law wanted her coincided temporally, more or less, with the beginning of the stress that her mother-in-law was experiencing.

The vision Mrs. Judd had of her mother-in-law and step-father-in-law lasted approximately a minute. The apparitions were opaque to light and appeared just as real as ordinary persons do, so much that, as already mentioned, Mrs. Judd stretched out her hand to greet the figures, at which point they vanished.

Mr. and Mrs. Judd emphasized in my interview with them that they had no knowledge whatever that Mr. Judd's mother and stepfather had left their community, much less that they were in trouble in the Gulf of California. This seems the more credible because the two families were not on speaking terms at the time. This particular episode, however, reunited the families. Mr. Judd's mother, after being rescued and brought back to her town, told both Mr. and Mrs. Judd that during her ordeal she had thought of her whole family, including them; the fact of being alienated from them had evidently weighed on her conscience as she contemplated the possibility of dying of starvation and dehydration, which she very nearly did. This, then, is another case in which the agent was focusing on the percipient.

Mrs. Osborne Leonard described in her autobiography an impression she had which partly developed into an imaged perception, but failed to do so completely. Her account follows:

> Early one evening while writing letters, a strong feeling of uneasiness came upon me, and then I mentally heard a voice saying distinctly, "Grace," which is my sister's name. Then, "Danger—danger—great danger."
>
> I felt as if I were surrounded by a large expanse of water. It seemed as if I were almost in it, with a sense of noise and confusion all around me, though I could see nothing except the blue water.
>
> My normal mind then became acutely active.
>
> Had I known what I know now, I should have endeavored to remain as passive as possible, so as to keep in exactly the same psychic condition as when I heard the first words, "Grace— danger," but I sat straight up in my chair and called out loud, "What is it? What has happened to Grace? Tell me, I *must* know." I was filled with an awful sense of tragedy and suddenly I heard the word "drowned."
>
> Immediately I felt certain that my sister was drowned. I was so sure about it that nothing would have shaken my certainty . . . (29, pp. 253-254).

Yet it turned out that Mrs. Leonard's sister had not drowned, but someone close (physically) to her sister had. She had been crossing the Atlantic during the days of submarine warfare in World War I. (This much Mrs. Leonard knew normally.) And at the very time of Mrs. Leonard's impression the ship on which her sister was a passenger had been fired at by a submarine. The torpedo had missed the ship but its explosion rocked the ship, giving some passengers an impression of a hit. A young man with whom Grace had been friendly during the voyage (and with whom she was standing on the deck at the time) jumped prematurely over the side of the ship which then raced ahead and he drowned. Grace was much disturbed by this tragedy and had kept repeating to herself afterwards the word "drowned."

Mrs. Leonard's experience started with an impression of

uneasiness. She then developed some accurate imagery, but at that point became engulfed by emotion made stronger by her mis-relating both it and the word "drowned" to her sister. This may have prevented her from developing an accurate picture of the whole episode.

I have already pointed out that solitude as such does not promote the development of additional detail in an impression experience. Rather, the maintenance of sustained introspective concentration seems important in this. This naturally is usually easier when one is alone since the stimuli of other persons may prevent or interrupt the desired state of concentration. Two experiences reported by Ian MacLaren (pseudonym for the Scottish preacher, the Reverend John Watson) illustrate the difference which solitude may make in such development. In one of these, Dr. Watson had a strong impulse to visit a particular family, but could not get the house number correct. He described the experience as follows:

> One afternoon . . . I made up my list of sick visits and started to overtake them. After completing the first, and while going along a main road, I felt a strong impulse to turn down a side street and call on a family living in it. The impulse grew so urgent that it could not be resisted, and I rang the bell, considering on the doorstep what reason I should give for an unexpected call. When the door opened it turned out that strangers now occupied the house, and that my family had gone to another address, which was in the same street but could not be given. This was enough, it might appear, to turn one from aimless visiting, but still the pressure continued as if a hand were drawing one and I set out to discover their new house, till I had disturbed four families with vain inquiries. Then the remembrance of my unmade and imperative calls came upon me, and I abandoned my fruitless quest with some sense of shame. Had a busy clergyman not enough to do without such a wild-goose chase?—and one grudged the time he had lost.
>
> Next morning the head of that household I had yesterday sought in vain came into my study with such evident sorrow on his face that one hastened to meet him with anxious inquiries. "Yes, we are in great trouble; yesterday our little one (a young

baby) took very ill and died in the afternoon. My wife was
utterly overcome by the shock, and we would have sent for you
at the time, but had no messenger. I wish you had been there—
if you had only known!"

"And the time?"

"About half-past three."

So I had known, but had been too impatient (43, p. 182).

At the time of this impression, the percipient was out in the
street and not in a situation where he could easily become receptive
to upwelling imagery. On another occasion, however, he had an
impression when alone in his study at home and this time he did
develop the further detail of an exact date. He described this experience in the following passage:

Some years ago I was at work one forenoon in my study
and was very busy, when my mind became distracted and I
could not think out my sermon. It was as if a side stream had
rushed into a river, confusing and discoloring the water; and
at last, when the confusion was over and the water was clear,
I was conscious of a new subject. Some short time before a
brother minister, whom I knew well and greatly respected, had
suffered some dissension in his congregation and had received
our sincere sympathy. He had not, however, been in my mind
that day, but now I found myself unable to think of anything
else. My imagination began to work in the case till I seemed,
in the midst of the circumstances, as if I were the sufferer. Very
soon a suggestion arose and grew into a commandment, that I
should offer to take a day's duty for my brother. At this point
I pulled myself together and resisted what seemed a vagrant
notion. "Was such a thing ever heard of—that for no reason save
a vague sympathy one should leave his own pulpit and undertake
another's work, who had not asked him and might not want
him?" So one turned to his manuscript to complete a broken
sentence, but could only write "Dear A.B." Nothing remained
but to submit to this mysterious dictation and compose a letter
as best one could, till the question of date arose. There I paused
and waited, when an exact day came up before my mind,
and so I concluded the letter. It was, however, too absurd to

send; and so, having rid myself of this irrelevancy, I threw the letter into the fire and set to work again; but all day I was haunted by the idea that my brother needed my help. In the evening a letter came from him, written that very forenoon, explaining that it would be a great service to him and his people if I could preach some Sunday soon in his church, and that, owing to certain circumstances, the service would be doubled if I could come on such and such a day; and it was my date! My course was perfectly plain, and I at once accepted his invitation under a distinct sense of a special call, and my only regret was that I had not posted my first letter (43, pp. 181-182).

To conclude this section on the relationship between impressions and additional details or imagery, I quote three published cases which depart somewhat from the usual process of development of additional details or imagery and report one new case that is also atypical in this respect. In the first case, reported in *Phantasms of the Living,* an impression was followed some hours later by the development of imagery in a dream:

When a boy about 14 years of age, I was in school in Edinburgh, my home being in the West of Scotland. A thoughtless boy, free from all care or anxiety, in the [cricket] "Eleven" of my school, and popular with my companions, I had nothing to worry or annoy me. I boarded with two old ladies, now both dead.

One afternoon—on the day previous to a most important cricket match in which I was to take part—I was overwhelmed with a most unusual sense of depression and melancholy. I shunned my friends and got "chaffed" for my most unusual dullness and sulkiness. I felt utterly miserable, and even to this day I have a most vivid recollection of my misery that afternoon.

I knew that my father suffered from a most dangerous disease in the stomach—a gastric ulcer—and that he was always more or less in danger, but I knew that he was in his usual bad health, and that nothing exceptional ailed him.

That same night I had a dream. I was engaged in the cricket match. I saw a telegram being brought to me while batting, and it told me that my father was dying, and telling

me to come home at once. I told the ladies with whom I boarded
what my dream had been, and told them how real the impression
was. I went to the ground, and was engaged in the game, batting,
and making a score. I saw a telegram being brought out, read it,
and fainted. I at once left for home, and found my father had
just died when I reached the house. The ulcer in the stomach
had suddenly burst about 4 o'clock on the previous day, and it
was about that hour that I had experienced the most unusual
depression I have described. The sensations I had on that afternoon have left a most clear and distinct impression on my mind,
and now, after the lapse of 15 years, I well remember my miserable feelings (18, Vol. 1, pp. 278-279; case 4 of Tabulation).

In the second case, also reported in *Phantasms of the Living,*
both impression and imagery occurred in a dream. A portion of the
percipient's account follows:

I then turned on my side to go to sleep again, and immediately felt a consciousness of a presence in the room, and
singular to state, it was not the consciousness of a live person, but
of a spiritual presence. . . . This may have been a part of the
dream, for I felt as if I were dozing off again to sleep; but it was
unlike any dream I ever had. I felt also at the same time a
strong feeling of superstitious dread, as if something strange and
fearful were about to happen. I was soon asleep again or unconscious, at any rate, to my surroundings. Then I saw two men
engaged in a slight scuffle; one fell fatally wounded—the other
immediately disappeared. I did not see the gash in the wounded
man's throat, but knew that his throat was cut. I did not recognize
him, either, as my brother-in-law. I saw him lying with his hands
under him, his head turned slightly to the left, his feet close
together . . . (18, Vol. 1, pp. 384-386).

The percipient's account continued with the narration of
additional details of his dream. He was at the time in Florida and
the details of his dream corresponded remarkably with the brutal
murder of his brother-in-law, who was then in Virginia where the
percipient's wife was visiting him at the time.

In the third case, reported by W. F. Prince, the general impression occurred *after* the more detailed image instead of before, as is usually the case. The percipient was Mme Antoinette Adamowski, a well-known pianist:

> [I had] a vivid premonition of receiving a letter from my brother in Poland. I had one day a distinct vision of his face bending over me on my awakening from a night's sleep, and said to myself that I would surely hear from him on that day. I had no reason to expect any message on that day, and it happened during the war, when whole months were passing without any communication reaching us from the other side, so that I had no news of my brother for a long time. I was not thinking of him particularly on that day, however. I was so sure to receive a letter, after my vision, that I was very much surprised when nothing came by the first two mails, and when I saw a letter in the box on my return from town in the evening, I took it in my hand with the absolute certainty that it was the one I expected. [It was.]

Prince made the following comments about the case:

> Mme Adamowski says that she clearly recollects saying to herself directly after the vision that she would get a letter that day. It is this curious accompanying conviction which gives the incident most of its value. This was the only time that she ever had an experience like this (44, p. 140).

Here one can find nothing in the image perceived by the percipient to indicate the content of the impression derived from it. She might well have interpreted the vision of her brother's face as indicating his illness or death. Instead, and for no apparent rational cause, she developed the strong and correct impression that she would receive a letter from him. It would seem, then, that half this "message" came as an imaged experience, half as an impression. Unfortunately, the account gives no information about the percipient's emotional state at the time, or about whether she was alone or in a situation which might have been favorable to the development of imaged perceptions.

In the following case, hitherto unpublished, the percipient first had a dream in which the agent figured and then immediately upon awaking an impression about his death. As in the case of Mme Adamowski, it would seem that here too half the "message" came as an imaged experience (dream), half in the form of an impression.

Case 35

The percipient in this case was Mrs. Penny Berendt of Warren, Michigan, who first mentioned the experience in a letter (undated, but written in 1965) to Dr. J. G. Pratt. Subsequently I continued investigation of the case by correspondence with Mrs. Berendt and other informants who corroborated or verified details. I have also had one telephone conversation with Mrs. Berendt. I shall quote first from her letter to Dr. Pratt:

> In 1963 my best friend's brother-in-law [Chester Williams], whom I only met twice, but liked very much, was found dead late in the afternoon. I had a dream about him and when I awoke between 7 and 7:30 A.M. I knew he was dead.
>
> I called my friend and asked her how her brother-in-law was. She said he was fine, so I told her about my dream and feeling when I awoke. By the way, I called my friend at 12:15 P.M. on her lunch hour. My friend said he [her brother-in-law] was to pick up his wife from the hospital because she had had a minor operation. When he did not pick up his wife, she called several times. They broke into the house very late that day and found him dead in bed.

In our telephone conversation Mrs. Berendt mentioned a few details of her dream in which Mr. Williams and also an owl had figured. I asked her to send me a detailed account of the dream and she replied in a letter dated September 26, 1969, from which I quote the following:

> My dream: It seemed that I was in the country walking with Chester [Williams]. There were many trees with dead leaves, some on the trees and many, many dry leaves on the ground.

The owl was, I would say, about two feet tall and alive, but did not move. It did not seem like an unusual dream. I can still see the owl as sure as I would see it if I saw it now, but the whole dream was that way. [Neither] Chester nor I touched the owl. It was just there. I saw the trees and leaves first. The owl was on the ground sitting up or how you would see a regular owl. I have never seen a real one outside of that dream. I can't remember any color except the natural color of the trees and leaves that are dead like in real life. The owl was brownish. It was all on our right side. He (Chester) motioned for me to turn to the left and Chester kept walking toward the trees and owl. I don't remember anything as I turned to go left.

When I awoke . . . that is when I received the impression without any thought to the dream. I mean the impression of knowing Chester was dead and not dying.

In an earlier letter dated August 10, 1969, Mrs. Berendt had said: "I woke up and said to my husband, 'Chester [Williams] is sick or will die.' " This suggested that she was slightly less positive about the agent's condition. In another letter, dated September 6, 1969, Mrs. Berendt described her emotional state at the time of the impression as follows:

The feeling I got was an awareness and a frightened feeling in the pit of my stomach. I felt a little sick. It was also a feeling that you would get if you were driving and someone would run in front of your car. . . . I was still feeling that way at my Aunt Marie's before going to work. She tried to make me feel better, but to no avail.

Mrs. Berendt's aunt, Mrs. Marie Karakashian, furnished a corroboration of Mrs. Berendt's dream and her concern about Chester Williams, although not of her specific impression that he had died. She wrote in a note dated September 8, 1969:

. . . I remember very well the morning of September 20, 1963, when Penny Berendt came over and told me about her dream; she was very upset because she had dreamt of an owl, and about a Mr. Chester Williams. I told her not to worry and after our coffee she left for work. Later the same day, she called up and told me Mr. Williams had passed away.

I wrote to Mr. Frank Berendt, the percipient's husband, and he furnished the following information in letters dated September 6 and September 23, 1969:

> My wife awoke early—7 or 8 A.M.—and mentioned to me in an anxious voice that Chester [Williams] died. I do not know the man.
> He was [thought to be] in good health at the time.
> I was informed [of the death of Chester Williams] late [that] afternoon by my son at 6 P.M.
> Chester [Williams] died September 20, 1963.
> My wife had met the man [only] briefly, so she had no knowledge of his health, or that he was going to die.

In a note dated September 30, 1969, Mr. Berendt assured me that the occasion in question was the only one on which his wife had told him Chester Williams had died.

Further information about the experience was furnished by Mrs. Virginia Kedich, Mrs. Berendt's best friend and the sister-in-law of the late Chester Williams. In a letter dated September 28, 1969, Mrs. Kedich answered the following questions:

Q. Was Chester Williams thought to be in good health at the time of his death, so that his death was quite unexpected?

A. Yes.

Q. How old was he when he died?

A. Sixty-three years.

Q. At about what time during the day was his body found?

A. The body was found approximately at 11:30 A.M., but I did not hear about his death until 1:30 or 2:00 P.M.

Q. At what time of day was he thought to have died?

A. Sometime between 7:00 and 8:00 A.M.

Q. Do you recall that Penny Berendt telephoned you around 12:30 P.M. on the day of Chester Williams' death? If so, do you remember what she asked you, or what you talked about?

A. I do remember Penny calling, because it was so unusual

for her to call at that time of day. She knew I worked, but always came home at 12:00 noon. She called to ask how my sister was feeling. I mentioned the fact that my sister was in the hospital . . . and was waiting for my brother-in-law (Chester) to take her home.

During my telephone conversation with Mrs. Berendt she explained that she had telephoned Mrs. Kedich to verify her impression and had asked her how the Williams were without saying openly that she thought Chester Williams was dead. At the time of this telephone call Chester Williams' body had been found, but Mrs. Kedich was not notified until later in the afternoon.

Mrs. Chester Williams was in the hospital waiting for her husband; and their daughter, thinking that her father was sleeping late, had not gone into his room before she went to work. Thus the fact of his death was not known until after 11:00 A.M. of September 20, 1963, although he was presumed to have died between 7:00 and 8:00 A.M. Mrs. Berendt was thus wrong in her statement (in her letter to Dr. Pratt) that Mr. Williams' body was found "late in the afternoon." However, she did not hear about the death until late in the day herself, and perhaps later mistakenly thought she had been told about it just as soon as the body was discovered.

Mrs. Helene (Chester) Williams wrote about the death of her husband and also about Mrs. Berendt's prior acquaintance with him in a letter dated September 28, 1969, from which I quote the following:

> As to your questions: My husband's death was sudden and unexpected. He was under a doctor's care only because of his age—sixty-three. . . . My husband died September 20, 1963. The coroner said that he died sometime before 7:00 or 7:30 [A.M.]. My daughter was home with him. She is a light sleeper and heard no sound. The door to his room was slightly opened; she closed it a little so as not to waken him while she was preparing to get ready for work. She did not look into his room. . . .
>
> To my knowledge Penny [Berendt] met my husband twice. [The first time], her remark to me was: "I like him. He has a nice, kind face." The second time was at a wake. My sister's husband passed away July [1963]. These are the only times. Be-

fore my husband died I believe I myself had met Penny three or four times.

I obtained from the Michigan Department of Public Health a photostatic copy of Mr. Chester Williams' death certificate. This document confirms the fact that Mr. Williams died on September 20, 1963, two and a half months short of his sixty-third birthday. Time of death is given as 8:00 A.M., at his home. The immediate cause of death was a coronary occlusion. These data confirm some of the principal statements made by the informants of the case. However, it appears from further facts given in the death certificate that Mr. Williams had suffered over the past five years from hypertensive cardiovascular disease, and had been seen by his physician (who apparently made the original diagnosis) just five days before his death. It is difficult to reconcile this with the statements of several of the informants to the effect that Mr. Williams was in "good health" at the time of his death, and especially with the statement of his widow that "he was under a doctor's care only because of his age . . ." On the other hand, Mr. Williams' meeting with his physician five days before his death may have been merely for a routine examination and it is certain that the physician gave no alarm about Mr. Williams' condition because if he had Mrs. Williams would not have described her husband's death as "unexpected."[2] It is further very unlikely that the percipient, Mrs. Berendt, who barely knew Mr. Williams, would have had any information about his cardiovascular disease; and even with this information, no one could normally predict just when the coronary occlusion would occur.

As mentioned in Mrs. Williams' letter, Mrs. Berendt, although she had seen Mr. Williams only twice, liked him very much. In the telephone conversation I had with her on September 20, 1969,

---

[2] After having read the copy of Mr. Williams' death certificate, I wrote to Mrs. Williams and asked her specifically whether her husband was thought to have hypertensive cardiovascular disease. She replied in a letter postmarked January 28, 1970, as follows: ". . . I was never informed by Dr. Strand [Mr. Williams' physician] or by my husband of his vascular condition. I was not aware of it. I too learned of it for the first time from the death certificate."

Mrs. Berendt explained to me that she had a strong impression when she met Chester Williams that he was a "wonderful man." He seemed kindly and gentle and reminded her of her father, of whom she was very fond, who had died when she was twelve years old.

Mrs. Berendt, like some of the other percipients in the cases reported in this monograph, has had numerous other apparently paranormal experiences. The first of these, unfortunately uncorroborated, occurred when she was three years old. It concerned her father and as it illustrates her attachment to him it seems relevant to the impression she had in 1963 of Mr. Williams' death since he reminded her of her father. Mrs. Berendt described it in her letter of 1965 to Dr. Pratt as follows: "My first experience was when I was three years old, in New York visiting relatives with my mother. My father was in Detroit being held up [by a thief] in our home when I started to cry and I didn't stop until we went home. My mother was shaken up. She used to tell me the story over and over. I told my mother that someone wanted Daddy's money and a gold watch."

Comment on this case: It seems likely that the resemblance between Mr. Williams and Mrs. Berendt's father was sufficient to make him, although a comparative stranger, a person of enough importance to Mrs. Berendt to permit her to become paranormally aware of his death.

Mrs. Berendt stated that she did not immediately connect her dream and her strong impression that Chester Williams had died. The dream, however, contains symbolism—e.g., of dead autumn leaves and turning in different directions—which could be interpreted as indicative of Mr. Williams' death. The important point is, I think, that the strong emotion of the impression was apparently not an accompaniment of the imagery of the dream. Here, then, is a case in which imagery with little or no emotion occurred initially, and then there followed strong emotion and an interpretative conviction that the impression referred to the death of a specific person.

In her letter of September 6, 1969, Mrs. Berendt gave a good description of the subjective experience of anxiety. The physical

symptoms she described ("frightened feeling in the pit of my stomach . . . felt a little sick") might also be among those experienced
by a person dying of a heart attack, as Mr. Williams did. We
cannot be certain of this, but this may be another case in which
the percipient shared some of the physical sensations of the dying
agent.

The illustrative cases of the first part of this section dem-
onstrate that in some impression experiences the percipient begins with a general impression of the agent and his situation, and
then goes on to coax up into consciousness additional specific
details. This moving from the general to the more precise is something that we also find in many sensitives, by which I mean persons
who have more than the usual number of paranormal experiences
and more than the usual control over them when they occur. I have
already mentioned the experiences of Gilbert Murray in getting
general impressions first and then specific details (33). Tenhaeff
has given other illustrative examples of the initial general impression
gotten by a sensitive followed by the coming into consciousness of
specific details (71). I myself have studied a subject who, working
with Zener cards, would confuse square and circle far more often
than expected by chance. She got the general impression of a hol-
low or enclosed area; she often knew the target was either a square
or a circle, but could not tell which it was.

THE RELATIVE IMPORTANCE OF PERCIPIENT AND AGENT
IN IMPRESSION EXPERIENCES

The data presented in Chapter II and the newly published
cases of this monograph indicate that the agent plays an important
part in the processes of the percipient's experience. In the first
place, the majority of impression cases occur when someone emotionally tied to the percipient is in serious distress of some kind.
This fact alone suggests that a *relationship,* not just an individual,
is necessary for such experiences to occur. In addition, the cases
show agent focusing as a frequent feature. Probably agent focusing
occurred even more frequently than it was recorded; the records
are sometimes scanty with regard to such a detail.

It is nevertheless certain that in many instances the agent was definitely *not* thinking of the percipient and yet the latter somehow gained knowledge about his situation. Moreover, even when the agent did focus on the percipient, this by itself does not mean that such focusing necessarily had any causal role in the percipient's experience. That it did, however, have some influence is strongly suggested by the correlation between agent focusing and action taken by the percipient. (This correlation was found not only in the cases analyzed in Chapter II, but also in the newly published cases of which I shall present a summary analysis in the next chapter.)

The importance of the percipient is brought out again in the observation that these experiences, although they may (so it would seem) occur to anyone, happen more often to some persons than to others. Thus Mrs. Hellström has had twelve impression experiences, Mrs. Heywood at least ten, and Mrs. Hurth six. And a considerable number of the other percipients reported several or more such experiences. But even for these more gifted persons, the experiences tended to occur more with certain individuals as agents than with others, again pointing up the importance of relationships rather than of specific individual powers.

Some cases with agent focusing that seem at first glance to be rather clear instances of telepathy may be instead examples of clairvoyance. The percipient's mind may scan the environment for danger to his (or her) loved ones and, when this is detected, "tunes in" and brings more details to the surface of consciousness. In such cases agent focusing could be a coincidental and inconsequential feature arising from the fact that the agent, when in distress, would naturally think of loved ones who would wish to help. In other experiences, however, the activity of the agent may play an important and decisive role. The cases so far published and analyzed indicate strongly the need for a careful examination of an even larger series in the hope of further clarifying the roles of the percipient, of the agent, and of the relationship between them.

SUMMARY OF CONCLUSIONS ABOUT THE PROCESSES OF
COMMUNICATION AS ILLUSTRATED BY IMPRESSION CASES

1. The same percipient may have impression experiences at one time and imaged experiences at another time.

2. Impression cases may consist of rather rich experiences in which a specific person is identified as in trouble, together with one or more additional details about his situation; and this information may be accompanied by emotions and impulses to action appropriate to the agent's situation.

3. *Formes frustes* of impression experiences may occur in which the percipient becomes aware only of an unusually strong emotion, a physical symptom, or an impulse toward action without any cognitive component in the experience.

4. Emotional and (other) physical components of the percipient's experience may take either one of two forms: He may imitate the agent's emotion or physical condition with corresponding or very similar symptoms; or he may *react* to his awareness (at unconscious levels sometimes) of the agent's distress by developing emotions or physical symptoms which do not resemble those of the agent. The percipient may develop a reactive emotion, e.g., depression with weeping, in response to the death of the agent without recognizing that the stimulus for this emotion has occurred in an extrasensory communication.

5. There is evidence that when action is taken by the percipient, it tends to inhibit the emergence of cognitive details in the experience. It is possible that strong emotions have a similarly inhibiting effect, but there is no evidence on this point.

6. If the agent focuses on the percipient during his (usually stressful) situation, this increases the likelihood that the percipient will act on his impression. But agent focusing is not positively correlated with the emergence of additional details in the percipient's experience.

7. Impression experiences tend to occur predominantly in percipients who are awake. Solitude as such does not tend to increase the number of details which emerge in an impression experience.

8. Nevertheless, when a percipient can achieve a steady state of concentrated introspection he can sometimes bring into consciousness additional details about the agent's situation.

Chapter Six

THE EVIDENCE FOR EXTRASENSORY PERCEPTION
FROM IMPRESSION CASES

Before taking up the final topic of the evidence for extra-sensory perception provided by impression cases, I will present a short analysis of the main features of the thirty-five hitherto unpublished cases presented in this monograph.

ANALYSIS OF THE THIRTY-FIVE NEW CASES

Although the series of cases published for the first time in this monograph contains four cases in which the impressions related to future events and one case without any identified agent, I am combining these cases with the others for this analysis.

Of the twenty-five percipients, six were males and sixteen females. As already mentioned, there was one case in which no agent was identifiable (Case 24); there were also nine cases in which two persons could have acted as agents. In the remaining twenty-five cases there were fourteen male agents and eleven female agents.

The relationships between percipients and agents in these cases show the same high frequency of close family connections found in the 160 cases analyzed in Chapter II. Of the thirty-four cases in which some agent could be identified, in all but ten agent and percipient were members of the same immediate family. In three instances the percipient was a more distant relative of the presumed agent (Cases 4, 14, and 26); in two instances the percipient was a friend or acquaintance of the agent (Cases 23 and 35); in another the percipient was a stranger to both possible agents (Case 27); and in four cases the agent was a friend attached to the percipient and rather dependent on her (Cases 16, 17, 18 and 19).

The themes of the related events in the thirty-five cases are divided as follows:

Death	6
Illness or accident	20
Not serious	9
	—
Total	35

In the high incidence of death, illness, and accidents among the themes of related events, this smaller series resembles the larger one analyzed in Chapter II.

The percipient identified the agent (or agents) in thirty of the thirty-four cases in which there was an agent. This incidence (90 per cent) of agent identification is much higher than that (65 per cent) of the 160 cases analyzed in Chapter II. I do not know any reason for this.

In nineteen of the cases the percipient took some action related to the impression (other than simply telling some unconnected person about it, or recording it) before having normal knowledge of the agent's situation.

In sixteen cases (out of thirty-four in which there was an identified agent) there was definite evidence that the agent was thinking of the percipient at the time of the latter's impression. (In several other cases it is very likely that the agent was doing so, but no definite information on the point emerged in the investigation.) This incidence (47 per cent) of agent focusing is much higher than that of the series analyzed in Chapter II, in which it was only approximately 29 per cent. The difference is perhaps due to my having specifically asked about this feature during my investigation of the cases.

Eleven of the sixteen cases with the agent focusing on the percipient belong to the group of nineteen cases in which the percipient took action in response to his impression, while only five belong to the group of sixteen in which the percipient did not take action. Thus, it can be seen that in this small series the tendency again emerges for agent focusing to correlate positively with action taken by the percipient. In contrast, however, to the larger series analyzed in Chapter II, the difference between the number of percipients taking action with and without agent focusing did not reach statistical significance.

Since the present new series of cases is small, I do not want to press the value of this analysis of its data. But the foregoing figures and other comparisons certainly show a rather close correspondence of characteristics to the much larger series analyzed in Chapter II.

The Strength of the Evidence for Extrasensory Perception from Impression Cases

I am willing to state that I think the corroborated cases of this monograph (as well as of the older series reviewed in Chapter II) are best interpreted in terms of extrasensory perception.[1] This does not mean that I think that any individual case provides *proof* of extrasensory processes, but simply that taking account of all the facts that I could assemble about these cases, extrasensory perception seems to me to be the best available present interpretation for them.

As can be seen from the reports, I engaged in extensive correspondence (often over several years) with the informants about details that might have betrayed some evidence of normal communication or chance coincidence in the cases. And I continued my probing, whenever possible, by interviewing the percipient and/or the agent or another firsthand witness in all but four of the thirty-five cases. During the course of my prolonged investigations I dropped two cases that I had originally thought strong enough for inclusion in this monograph. In one case the percipient wavered in her statements about just what she had experienced. In the other case the percipient gave a detailed description of what seemed like an excellent example of an impression experience with

---

[1] From this statement I except Case 13 where there was a much greater possibility that the percipient's experience coincided with the related event by chance than in the other corroborated cases.

some physical symptoms and visual imagery. The agent of this case, whom the percipient had said he had tried to telephone, was unable to corroborate it. Furthermore, she furnished a letter written by the percipient to her just after the time he said he had had his experience and it contained no mention of it; the case may have occurred as he said it did, but the evidence as a whole made me think he had later had an illusion of memory.

It is nevertheless quite possible that I have overlooked some important details in one or more cases which, if known about, would disqualify a paranormal interpretation. But as the number of cases grows, this possibility becomes less and less reasonable as grounds for discounting all of them. If we add the present series to the series analyzed in Chapter II, we have 195 cases in all. For most of these there are at least two witnesses and for many, three or more witnesses. The cases have had many different and independent investigators. It seems to me most improbable that all these informants would have mixed up their observations and memories or that all these investigators would have been completely misled. It is surely much more likely that at least in some cases the main events corresponded closely enough with the reports published so that the one represents the other accurately enough for judgment and interpretation. If so, we can regard at least some of these cases as being examples of extrasensory perception.

But the cases do not gain weight as evidence of paranormal processes only from the assessment of each one individually. They derive strength also from their conformity to patterns and from fitting into natural groups similar or allied to other groups of cases. We can discern these patterns and alliances in several relationships.

There is, first of all, the similarity of main features between the small newly published series and the much larger series analyzed in Chapter II. And we also find resemblances in patterns between the series of impression cases and other series of spontaneous cases illustrated in the comparisons of Table 4. These similarities of pattern suggest that the cases of each series are members of some larger natural group.

It seems to me also that the impression cases merge with

allied experiences as naturally occurring phenomena should do. We have seen how at one extreme of the range of experience, impression cases may occur with pure feeling or pure action as the sole component of the experience, which is void of any cognitive content. At the other extreme, however, we find impression cases which initially include, or which develop, additional details of information and actual imagery so that they thus merge in form with hallucinatory and dream experiences.

This evidence of group membership and shading into other types of experiences is not by itself evidence of paranormality. But it is evidence, in my opinion, of authenticity, for it is most unlikely that we should see these patterns if the cases had been individually contrived with fraud or fantasy by alleged percipients who had no contact with each other. And if we strengthen our conviction about authenticity in the cases as a group, we gain considerably in justifying a paranormal interpretation of the individual cases. For I think there can be little doubt that if the cases occurred as reported, then the interpretation that they include extrasensory perception would seem to be the most plausible one. Other explanations gain force only through casting doubt on the memories, capacities for observation, or integrity of the main informants.

Finally, I wish to draw attention to certain experiments which have studied in the laboratory the kinds of communications that impression cases exemplify in everyday life; namely, the communication of "pure" feeling or emotion. I refer to the work of Figar (14) and later of Dean (8), who have obtained evidence of extrasensory perception solely expressed in changes in the circulation of the percipient as measured by the plethysmograph. Such experimental evidence of the stimulation of the physiological accompaniments of emotion (without associated cognitive effects) does not make the spontaneous impression cases more authentic, but it does make them more credible by providing another type of demonstration (and a more controlled one) that extrasensory communication may occur when the only outward manifestation is a change of emotion in the percipient.

If, as I believe, impression cases provide important evidence of extrasensory perception, then we can say one thing more. This is that such experiences almost certainly occur very much more frequently than most persons now realize, and that they may have more influence on our conduct than we realize. For impression experiences, lacking detail as they usually do, may be quite difficult to recognize and verify. Hallucinatory and imaged dream experiences (with their greater detail) are usually more impressive to the percipient. This may account for the greater frequency of dream experiences in published series of spontaneous cases. It is altogether probable that important unrecognized exchanges of feelings through extrasensory processes are occurring all the time to most of us and perhaps significantly influencing our emotions and behavior.

That we are linked to each other in hidden ways that are, at least sometimes, powerfully influential has been the contention of mystics of all ages and places. It was also hinted at or explicitly stated as a conviction by several pioneers in psychical research such as Myers, James, and Bergson. And it was a conclusion reached by Warcollier at the end of his book reporting the results of his experiments with telepathy (78). To believe in some universal binding that joins us all is not, of course, to deny that for most of us this union is never manifested consciously. But even if we can only observe it occasionally, and usually between persons united by love and during a special crisis to one of them, this should arouse our curiosity and our efforts to find out why this is so—why the union is latent for most of us and why it does sometimes reach expression in a few of us. At any rate, the evidence pointing to such pervasive interactions between human beings surely justifies a much more extensive survey and analysis of impression experiences than the present monograph has provided.

Such further studies will certainly show that many impressions initially attributable to extrasensory perception have simple, normal explanations. But I am convinced that they will also show that some intuitions, sudden changes of feelings, and even physical symptoms that are now given no explanation or dismissed as fortuitous include processes of extrasensory communication. Such clarifications cannot fail to increase our still very small understanding of the nature of human personality.

REFERENCES

1. BARBER, T. X. "Death by Suggestion: A Critical Note." *Psychosomatic Medicine,* Vol. 23, 1961, 152-155.
2. BARRETT, W. F., AND OTHERS. "Third Report of the Committee on Mesmerism." *Proc.* S.P.R., Vol. 2, 1884, 12-23.
3. BARROWS, C. M. "Suggestion without Hypnotism: An Account of Experiments in Preventing or Suppressing Pain." *Proc.* S.P.R., Vol. 12, 1896-97, 21-44.
4. CALLAWAY, E., AND DEMBO, D. "Narrowed Attention: A Psychological Phenomenon that Accompanies a Certain Physiological Change." *Archives of Neurology and Psychiatry,* Vol. 79, 1958, 74-90.
5. CANNON, W. B. "Voodoo Death." *American Anthropologist,* Vol. 44, 1942, 169-181.
6. DALE, L. A. "Spontaneous Cases." *Journal* A.S.P.R., Vol. 46, 1952, 31-35.
7. DALE, L. A., WHITE, R. A., AND MURPHY, G. "A Selection of Cases from a Recent Survey of Spontaneous ESP Phenomena." *Journal* A.S.P.R., Vol. 56, 1962, 3-47.
8. DEAN, E. D. "Plethysmograph Recordings as ESP Responses." *International Journal of Neuropsychiatry,* Vol. 2, 1966, 439-446.

9. *Demographic Yearbook, 1967.* New York: United Nations, 1968.

10. EHRENWALD, J. *Telepathy and Medical Psychology.* New York: W. W. Norton, 1948.

11. ————. "Telepathy and the Child-Parent Relationship." *Journal* A.S.P.R., Vol. 48, 1954, 43-55.

12. EISENBUD, J. "The Use of the Telepathy Hypothesis in Psychotherapy." In G. Bychowski and J. L. Despert (Eds.), *Specialized Techniques in Psychotherapy.* New York: Basic Books, 1952.

13. "Excerpta." *Journal* S.P.R., Vol. 42, 1963, 161.

14. FIGAR, S. "The Application of Plethysmography to the Objective Study of So-called Extrasensory Perception." *Journal* S.P.R., Vol. 40, 1959, 162-172.

15. FODOR, N. "Telepathy—Inhibitive, Cathartic and Malignant." *International Journal of Parapsychology,* Vol. 1, 1959, 125-130.

16. GIBSON, E. P. "An Examination of Motivation as Found in Selected Cases from *Phantasms of the Living.*" *Journal* A.S.P.R., Vol. 36, 1944, 83-105.

17. GREEN, C. "Analysis of Spontaneous Cases." *Proc.* S.P.R., Vol. 53, 1960, 97-161.

18. GURNEY, E., MYERS, F. W. H., AND PODMORE, F. *Phantasms of the Living.* London: Trübner, 1886. (2 vols.)

19. GUYON, J. M. B. DE LA M. *Autobiography.* (The Exemplary Life of the Pious Lady Guyon translated from her own account in the original French by T. L. Brooke.) Philadelphia: Joseph Cruikshank, 1804.

20. HEYWOOD, R. "Case of Rapport between Mother and Daughter." *Journal* S.P.R., Vol. 42, 1963, 187-189.

21. ————. *The Infinite Hive: A Personal Record of Extrasensory Experiences.* London: Chatto and Windus, 1964. (American edition published in 1964 by Dutton under the title *ESP: A Personal Memoir.*)

22. ————. "An Apparently Telepathic Impression of Illness." *Journal* S.P.R., Vol. 44, 1968, 237-239.

23. HODGSON, R. "Case." *Journal* S.P.R., Vol. 5, 1891, 54-61.

24. ————. "Case Report." *Journal* S.P.R., Vol. 7, 1896, 195-196.

25. HYSLOP, J. H. "A Case of Premonition." *Journal* A.S.P.R., Vol. 1, 1907, 165-168.

26. ————. "Miscellaneous Experiences." *Journal* A.S.P.R., Vol. 8, 1914, 121-160.

27. JUNG, C. G. *Erinnerungen, Traüme, Gedanken.* (Recorded and edited by Aniela Jaffé.) Zurich: Rascher Verlag, 1963. (American edition published in 1963 by Pantheon Books under the title *Memories, Dreams, Reflections.*)

28. LAMON, W. H. *Recollections of Abraham Lincoln, 1847-1865.* Chicago: McClurg, 1895.

29. LEONARD, G. O. *My Life in Two Worlds.* London: Cassell, 1931.

30. LUKIANOWICZ, H. "Hallucinations à Trois." *Archives of General Psychiatry,* Vol. 1, 1959, 322-331.

31. MATTHEWS, F. B. "An Account of an Outbreak of Religious Hallucination in the Bahamas, West Indies." *Journal* S.P.R., Vol. 2, 1886, 485-488.

32. MEDLICOTT, R. W. "An Inquiry into the Significance of Hallucinations with Special Reference to their Occurrence in the Sane." *International Record of Medicine,* Vol. 171, 1958, 664-677.

33. MURRAY, G. "Presidential Address." *Proc.* S.P.R., Vol. 49, 1952, 155-169.

34. MYERS, F. W. H. "The Subliminal Consciousness." *Proc.* S.P.R., Vol. 8, 1892, 333-535.

35. ————. "The Subliminal Consciousness." *Proc.* S.P.R., Vol. 9, 1893, 3-128.

36. ————. "The Subliminal Self." *Proc.* S.P.R., Vol. 11, 1895, 334-593.

37. ————. *Human Personality and its Survival of Bodily Death.* London: Longmans, Green, 1903. (2 vols.)

38. NICOL, J. F., AND NICOL, B. H. "Investigation of a Curious 'Hunch.'" *Journal* A.S.P.R., Vol. 52, 1958, 24-34.

39. OKEN, D., AND OTHERS. "Stress Response in a Group of Chronic Psychiatric Patients." *Archives of General Psychiatry,* Vol. 3, 1960, 451-466.

40. OSTY, E. *Supernormal Faculties in Man.* (Trans. by S. de Brath.) London: Methuen, 1923.

41. PRASAD, J., AND STEVENSON, I. "A Survey of Spontaneous Psychical Experiences in School Children of Uttar Pradesh, India." *International Journal of Parapsychology,* Vol. 10, 1968, 241-261.

42. PRINCE, W. F. "A Group of Supposed Premonitions and Monitions." *Journal* A.S.P.R., Vol. 12, 1918, 248-281.

43. ————. *Noted Witnesses for Psychic Occurrences.* Boston: Boston Society for Psychic Research, 1928.

44. ————. "Human Experiences: Being a Report of the Results of a Questionnaire and a Discussion of Them." *Bulletin* XIV, Boston Society for Psychic Research, 1931, 1-331.

45. ————. "The Sinclair Experiments Demonstrating Telepathy." *Bulletin* XVI, Boston Society for Psychic Research, 1932, 1-138.

46. RENDALL, V. H. "Case." *Journal* S.P.R., Vol. 5, 1891, 172.

47. RHINE, L. E. "Subjective Forms of Psi Experiences." *Journal of Parapsychology,* Vol. 17, 1953, 77-114.

48. ————. "Frequency of Types of Experience in Spontaneous Precognition." *Journal of Parapsychology,* Vol. 18, 1954, 93-123.

49. ————. "Psychological Processes in ESP Experiences. Part I. Waking Experiences." *Journal of Parapsychology,* Vol. 26, 1962, 88-111.

50. ————. "Comparison of Subject Matter of Intuitive and Realistic ESP Experiences." *Journal of Parapsychology,* Vol. 29, 1965, 96-108.

51. ————. "Hallucinatory Experiences and Psychosomatic Psi." *Journal of Parapsychology,* Vol. 31, 1967, 111-134.

52. ROBERTSON, C. L. "Case Report." *Journal* S.P.R., Vol. 8, 1897, 45-48.

53. ROSE, R. *Living Magic.* New York: Rand McNally, 1956.

54. Rush, J. H. "New Directions in Parapsychological Research." *Parapsychological Monographs No. 4.* New York: Parapsychology Foundation, 1964.

55. Saltmarsh, H. F. "Report on Cases of Apparent Precognition." *Proc.* S.P.R., Vol. 42, 1934, 49-103.

56. Sannwald, G. "Statistische Untersuchungen an Spontanphänomenen." *Zeitschrift für Parapsychologie und Grenzgebiete der Psychologie,* Vol. 3, 1959, 59-71.

57. ————. "Zur Psychologie Paranormaler Spontanphänomene: Motivation, Thematik und Bezugspersonen 'okkulter' Erlebnisse." *Zeitschrift für Parapsychologie und Grenzgebiete der Psychologie,* Vol. 3, 1959, 149-183.

58. Schmeidler, G. R. "Are There Two Kinds of Telepathy?" *Journal* A.S.P.R., Vol. 55, 1961, 87-97. (See also "Evidence for Two Kinds of Telepathy." *International Journal of Parapsychology,* Vol. 3, 1961, 5-48.)

59. Schwarz, B. E. "Possible Telesomatic Reactions." *Journal of the Medical Society of New Jersey,* Vol. 64, 1967, 600-603.

60. Searles, H. "The Schizophrenic's Vulnerability to the Therapist's Unconscious Processes." *Journal of Nervous and Mental Disease,* Vol. 127, 1958, 247-262.

61. Sidgwick, E. M. "Phantasms of the Living. . . ." *Proc.* S.P.R., Vol 33, 1923, 23-429.

62. ————. "Review of Upton Sinclair's *Mental Radio.*" *Proc.* S.P.R., Vol. 39, 1931, 343-346.

63. Sinclair, U. *Mental Radio.* London: Werner Laurie, 1951. (First published in 1930.)

64. Stevenson, I. "A Review and Analysis of Paranormal Experiences Connected with the Sinking of the *Titanic.*" *Journal* A.S.P.R., Vol. 54, 1960, 153-171.

65. ————. "Correspondence." *Journal of Parapsychology,* Vol. 25, 1962, 59-64.

66. ————. "Seven More Paranormal Experiences Associated with the Sinking of the *Titanic.*" *Journal* A.S.P.R., Vol. 59, 1965, 211-225.

67. ————. "Correspondence." *Journal* A.S.P.R., Vol. 61, 1967, 78-80.

68. ————. "Single Physical Symptoms as Residues of an Earlier Response to Stress." *Annals of Internal Medicine,* Vol. 70, 1969, 1231-1237.

69. ————. "Precognition of Disasters." *Journal* A.S.P.R., Vol. 64, 1970, 187-210.

70. TANAGRAS, A. "Psychophysical Elements in Parapsychological Traditions." *Parapsychological Monographs No. 7.* New York: Parapsychology Foundation, 1967.

71. TENHAEFF, W. H. C. *Hellsehen und Telepathie.* (German translation of *Telepathie en Helderziendheid.*) Gütersloh, Germany: C. Bertelsmann Verlag, 1962.

72. THURSTON, H. *The Physical Phenomena of Mysticism.* London: Burns Oates, 1952.

73. TRETHOWAN, W. H., AND CONLON, M. F. "The Couvade Syndrome." *British Journal of Psychiatry.* Vol. 111, 1965, 57-66.

74. TYRRELL, G. N. M. "The 'Modus Operandi' of Paranormal Cognition." *Proc.* S.P.R., Vol. 48, 1946, 65-120.

75. ————. *The Personality of Man.* London: Penguin Books, 1947.

76. VERRALL, MRS. A. W. "Report on a Series of Experiments in 'Guessing.'" *Proc.* S.P.R., Vol. 29, 1918, 64-110.

77. *Vital Statistics of the United States, 1966.* Washington, D. C.: Department of Health, Education and Welfare. Government Printing Office, 1968.

78. WARCOLLIER, R. *La Télépathie: Recherches Expérimentales.* Paris: Librairie Félix Alcan, 1921. (See also *Experimental Telepathy.* Boston: Boston Society for Psychic Research, 1938.)

79. WENZL, A. "Empirische und theoretische Beiträge zur Erinnerungsarbeit bei erschwerter Wortfindung." *Arch. Ges. Ps.,* Vol. 85, 1932, 181-218; Vol. 97, 1936, 294-318.

80. WEST, D. J. *Psychical Research Today.* London: Duckworth, 1954.

81. ————. "Presidential Address: ESP the Next Step." *Proc.* S.P.R., Vol. 54, 1965, 185-202.

82. WHITE, R. A. "A Comparison of Old and New Methods of Response to Targets in ESP Experiments." *Journal* A.S.P.R., Vol. 58, 1964, 21-56.

83. WICKES, F. G. "Three Illustrations of the Power of the Projected Image." In *Studien zur Analytischen Psychologie C. G. Jungs*. i Band. Beiträge aus Theorie und Praxis. Zurich: Rascher Verlag, 1955.

INDEX

This is the first collection of telepathic impression cases to be printed in almost eighty years. It includes thirty-five new cases never published before. These are reported in great detail and are studied thoroughly by one of the nation's most authoritative parapsychologists. Impression cases are those which involve no visual images, but only a vague impression that something is happening to another person who is a considerable distance away. The one who receives the impression, the percipient, is usually emotionally close to the other person, the target. Some of the impressions include strong emotions, and some include physical symptoms that correspond with the experiences of the distant target person. Often the receiver has a strong impulse to go to the help of the person he senses as being in need of him. In most cases the target person is in some serious situation—seriously ill, injured in an accident, or close to death.

This book first summarizes 160 cases previously published and examined for authenticity. Reports on the thirty-five new cases follow. These reports, thoroughly investigated by the author, include statements corroborating each percipient's claim that he had an impression of the target's experience before he was actually informed of it. The reports also contain statements from the target persons or other informants who were involved in the situation. Target persons, in fact, are given new importance in these thirty-five cases. Previous studies have neglected them because of the emphasis given to the percipient. Following the reports is a valuable list of reading sources for further study of telepathic impressions.